# AN EGO-PSYCHOLOGICAL APPROACH
# TO CHARACTER ASSESSMENT

# AN EGO-PSYCHOLOGICAL
# APPROACH TO
# CHARACTER ASSESSMENT

*ERNST PRELINGER and CARL N. ZIMET*
· · ·

*With the collaboration of Roy Schafer and Max Levin*

THE FREE PRESS OF GLENCOE

COLLIER-MACMILLAN LIMITED, LONDON

# ACKNOWLEDGMENTS

This co-authored study is supported by Grant M-3642 from the National Institutes of Mental Health and by a grant from the National Association for Mental Health.

Dr. Peter Lenrow's assistance in the supervision of the data analysis and Mrs. Grace Goldin's help in the preparation of the manuscript are gratefully acknowledged.

# CONTENTS

# AN EGO-PSYCHOLOGICAL APPROACH
## TO CHARACTER ASSESSMENT

# 1
# INTRODUCTION AND
# HISTORICAL SURVEY

This study emerges from the authors' interest in ego development and character structure. The assessment technique described here was developed as an aid to understanding the complexities of personality, not as a tool to predict behavior in certain situations or under particular circumstances. Unfortunately, the term "assessment" has largely become synonymous with efforts to predict behavior for purposes of selection and/or validation. Such studies should be clearly differentiated from those focused on character in its own right; a distinction perhaps best expressed in the two designations, *assessment for* and *assessment of*. The former would refer to studies of a predictive type, whereas the intrinsic interest of the latter would be to understand the many facets of a personality.

The *assessment of* study reported here does not approach personality from a "buckshot" point of view, covering a multiplicity of variables which can be tapped, often without a comprehensive or theoretical framework and often while tied to one particular method, e.g., a questionnaire. As described in greater detail below, our procedure is not method-centered; and our rating scales, oriented toward *assessment of*, are based on deductive variables that originate in a theory.

More specifically, our assessment procedure was developed as part of a joint research investigation into values, the development of ego identity during late adolescence, and the relationship of aspects of character to interpersonal interaction in groups. All these research problems concerned with ego functioning required a careful prior assessment of the character structure of the subjects who participated in them.

Investigation into patterns of ego functions can be carried out meaningfully only after the subjects' degree and quality of personal development have been assessed and summarized in terms as objective as possible. The assessment procedure reported in the following pages uses psychoanalytically defined variants of character structure, each of which includes particular patterns of ego defense, primary drive and superego conflicts, modes of thought, interpersonal relationships, and different qualities of the self concept.

The assessment schedule that was devised consists of 78 five-point rating scales which can be used in summarizing information from various sources (psychological tests, interviews, etc.) in which idiographic information is elicited. The rating system and its use, as well as some evidence of its reliability and validity, will be discussed after examining the merits of our particular approach to assessment as compared to other assessment schemes in the literature.

Methods of psychological assessment have developed rapidly in recent years, as indeed have many phases of the psychology of personality. Twenty-five years ago, psychologists as well as sophisticated laymen thought of assessment of psychological functioning in the individual almost exclusively as intelligence testing, plus, possibly, the evaluation of motor skills. Psychiatrists and psychoanalysts, on the other hand, have been assessing individual psychological functioning by use of clinical methods for a relatively long time. In clinical interviews they observed the patient's manner of expressing thoughts and feelings, style of speech and behavior, and this led to a variety of diagnostic conceptions and prognostic formulations. Thus practitioners learned a great deal about the complexity, the hierarchy and intricate organization of human personality, and about the subtle and powerful forces operating within it. How the interview was carried out, whether probing, directed, or permissive, and how its content was interpreted depended in large measure, as it still does today, on the theoretical orientation and to some extent on the personal predilections of the clinician. By his psychodynamic insights and his structural concepts, Freud furthered the comprehension of personality and vastly enriched the diagnostic judgments of his time. He emphasized that the complex, often nonconscious determinants of personality could only be understood by a flexible and detailed inquiry. The work was largely limited to the evaluation of disordered individuals, since the psychiatrists and psychoanalysts engaged in it were primarily interested in understanding and treating psychopathology.

Psychoanalytic thinking provided the basis for the development of projective techniques which subsequently led to the development of psychological tests offering new dimensions for the understanding of the disordered personality. Only recently, however, have psychoanalysts and clinical psychologists become interested in applying their clinical skills to the assessment of nondisturbed individuals and to the study of processes involved in normal development and normal functioning.

One of the central issues that has emerged in personality research is how best to summarize and express the information that has been collected. Certainly among the more clinically minded there is little doubt that a descriptive evaluation provides the "richest" presentation of the data. However, in research projects involving large numbers of subjects the descriptive approach becomes more burdensome than useful, and has to give way to a less integrated and also less subtle and sensitive method to make statistical manipulation possible.

To study an individual personality, or certain aspects of that personality, one must somehow be able to encompass it, to codify or categorize it. An almost unlimited range and variety of categories might be chosen for such a project. Since, theoretically, an unlimited number of categories could be chosen or omitted, a relevant decision must depend on the kind of study being undertaken. The study's breadth (atomistic *vs.* global), depth (behavorial traits *vs.* conscious and nonconscious dynamics of behavior), and most of all the purpose of the study (understanding *vs.* prediction and/or validation) must determine the approach. If the focus is to be upon descriptive assessment per se (i.e., giving as lifelike a portrait of the individual as is possible), rather than on prediction or validation, the categories to be included will be extensive. This must be because conscious and nonconscious motivations, atomistic and global considerations are important to a complete account of individual functioning. Global, configurational assessment in terms of a number of variables is a close but objectified approximation to a thorough clinical evaluation.

Any configurational assessment, however, implying some kind of organization of variables (hierarchical, or in terms of clusters) requires some preconception of personality; in other words, a theory. Not enough attention has been given to making explicit the relationship between assessment procedures that have been reported, on the one hand, and assessors' conception of personality on the other. Failure to state what should be encompassed in a complete assessment of a personality tends to obscure the degree to which assessment studies have fallen short of an adequate treatment of the complexity and richness of the personality. Furthermore, using categories without the conceptual backing of a theoretical system can only lead to an assembly of data referring back to tests or specific behavioral traits previously described as the "buckshot" approach. The choice of a particular theory from which to derive categories for ordering assessment information is thus important, and the following considerations affecting the choice of a particular theory suggest themselves:

1. The system should be general enough to encompass all the dimensions of personality; that is, it should include phenotypic and genotypic considerations, behavior traits and fantasy trends, impulses and their controls, resources and limitations.

2. It should be explicit enough to allow the development of categories clearly related to theoretical variables, rather than to isolated clinical phenomena, or to simple diagnostic labels.

3. It should be well known and accepted by a reasonably large group of workers in the field.

4. It must correspond to the orientation of the researcher or researchers involved.

To the writers, psychoanalytic theory suggested itself because of its generality, because it encompasses normal development as well as abnormal behavior, because it has demonstrated its capacity to stimulate experimental research, and because it is widely known if not generally accepted by psychology and psychiatry; but most important, because it is acceptable to this research group as a theoretical framework.

None of the assessment approaches developed to date provides a comprehensive system of personality assessment within the framework of a unified theory. Only Murray's system (1938) and that of Stern, Stein, and Bloom (1956), which grew out of it, come close to a generally accepted theoretical framework. Murray attempted to integrate psychoanalytic theory with aspects of cultural anthropology and Jungian, Gestalt, and academic psychology. The only work prior to Murray's dealing with the application of clinical techniques for evaluating nondisturbed individuals was by Simoneit (1935), who used such methods in selecting officers for the German army. The publication of *Explorations in Personality* (Murray, 1938) laid the cornerstone for most of the subsequent sophisticated work in clinical assessment. In it he introduced the term "personology," which stood for the complete study of the individual personality. He emphasized the organic whole, standing firmly by the point of view that any single segment of behavior cannot be understood in isolation. Murray borrowed heavily from the psychoanalytic thinking of that day with its emphasis on infancy and early childhood as the primary determinants of later functioning. He accepted fully the existence of unconscious motivation and was interested in its expression through free, imaginative verbalization, via the Thematic Apperception Test which he developed. Many other devices for the evaluation of personality are described in *Explorations in Personality,* all reflecting his orientation: he believes that the understanding of human behavior will not develop out of the study of the rat or other favorite experimental animals of the psychologists, but rather through the complex evaluation of the individual.

Ten years later *Assessment of Men* was published (1948), a work very much in the Murray tradition, and since that time many other clinical assessment studies have been completed. Most of them, however, could more aptly be termed prediction studies rather than evaluations of personality, since their object was to forecast performance in certain defined situations or in certain roles: clinical psychologist (Kelly and Fiske, 1951), psychiatrist (Holt and Luborsky, 1958), spy or saboteur (*Assessment of Men*, 1948), theological student and teacher trainee (Stern, Stein, and Bloom, 1956).

Assessment in these studies is as inclusive or narrow, as depth-oriented or phenotypical, as specific or wide-ranging as the prediction demands. There have been few attempts at general assessment of the varieties and subtleties of the human personality. Instead, the aim has been to extract common characteristics from the personality structure of different individuals. Predictions are usually derived through inferences as to how these common or nomothetic constructs will interact with known or supposed properties of the situation. Such predictions encounter difficulties because they involve hazardous generalizations from a specific aspect of personality to behavior in an often unanalyzed situation. Thorough analyses of the situation, such as job requirements, must be made in predictive projects. Stern, Stein, and Bloom (1956) recognized this problem when they studied, in addition to the personality, the environment in which the individual was to act. The frequently poor results from predictive or validational studies have been cited by Meehl (1954), Cronbach (1956), Sarbin (1943), and others to derogate the role of clinical judgment. Holt (1958) divides predictive assessment studies into the "pure actuarial," the "naive clinical" and the "sophisticated clinical." In reviewing assessment studies, Taft (1959) separated them into the naive empirical, the global, and the analytic type of assessment strategies. For our purposes Holt's pure actuarial, or, to employ Taft's label, the naive empirical approach, will be omitted from this discussion since it only utilizes objective test data to predict specified performance on the basis of statistical processes.

In Holt's naive clinical, as in Taft's global approach, predictions of behavior or personality functioning are directly derived from assessment protocols. The assessors rely on clinical, intuitive processes without any mediating strategy. "Mediating constructs" is meant here as a set of concepts devised by the assessor, of variables considered as important: how they are interrelated and how the subjects' test performance, interview material, and behavior may be categorized in terms of these variables. That is, a set of specific categories and concepts about how they are interrelated serves to mediate between the raw diagnostic data and the prediction of behavior.

The presence of mediating constructs, together with pilot studies, job analysis, and cross validation when appropriate and feasible, are what led Holt to classify a study as "sophisticated clinical" rather than "naive clinical." He points out that objectivity, organization and scientific method should be introduced wherever possible into the planning, gathering, and analysis of the data, but that the clinician himself must make the final organization and interpretation. At this point it might be useful to review briefly some of the major assessment studies that followed Murray's in terms of their use of naive clinical and sophisticated clinical approaches.

The OSS study (*Assessment of Men*, 1948) is an example of a clinical-intuitive procedure in which intervening variables were not formulated. Each rater had to decide on the basis of information available to him whether the assessee could function well in the types of work likely to come up in Secret Service assignments. These types of work were often unknown to the assessor, or, if outlined in detail, were frequently changed at a later date. The variety of possible assignments was equalled only by the variety of cultural background of the candidates.

A follow-up study was undertaken to determine the effectiveness of the predictions, but because of assignment changes and the difficulty of evaluating the field situation, meaningful results were sparse. Nevertheless many of the assessors, particularly those involved in designing the program, were very enthusiastic about the value of these assessment procedures.

The major study following the OSS work was the Clinical Psychology Assessment Project (Kelly and Fiske, 1951). Methodologically, this study might be considered of the "sophisticated clinical" type. The central concern of this large-scale undertaking, in which 280 students were examined, was the selection of trainees for the Veterans Administration Clinical Psychology Program. As in the OSS study, here too the emphasis was not on obtaining a thorough evaluation of the individual as such; the purpose was to study the validity of many psychological tests, interviews and questionnaires, and to develop criterion techniques for success in training and in the performance of professional work. The researchers were aware of the importance of mediating constructs, and formulated a list of personality variables. Unfortunately, these were compiled without any attempt to derive them from any established theoretical framework. The fact that criteria of success in clinical psychology were mostly unknown in 1948, as they largely are today, did not deter the researchers from setting up such criteria.

Their approach to the predictive problem was eclectic. Objective and projective tests, subjective and quantitative procedures were employed to rate the variables. The latter consisted of a series of personal traits, of which 22 were descriptive of the subject, 10 were evaluative judgments of broader underlying personality variables, and 11 were skill variables related to the future performance of each candidate as a clinical psychologist. All ratings were made on eight-point scales. Each staff member who evaluated the subjects was urged to use the personality theory or theories he found most acceptable and was permitted to formulate the dynamics of his cases in any manner he wished. Knowing what we do about diverse models and theories of personality, it seems most probable that great differences would appear in the evaluation of the subjects. Kelly and Fiske (1951), in explaining the failure of the project, state that the diagnostician seems satisfied with clinical idiographic descriptions and is rather neglectful about making good predictions. It appears to us that in predictive assessment projects the reverse is more likely to be the case; that is, the reseacher-clinician is much more interested in prediction—the concern of his study—than in the more basic issue, that of a thorough comprehension of an individual personality.

The results of this project showed that only the Miller Analogies Test and the Strong Vocational Interest Blank had any predictive value. The former correlated .47 with ratings on academic performance, the latter .43 with faculty ratings on research competence. There is general agreement that the weakest part of the study was once again the criterion problem, that is, what specific performances to use as criteria of "successful" clinical work. In general, the work did not further illuminate the issue of personality assessment per se.

Certain assessment projects might best be called criterion-focused studies. This type is best exemplified by the work of Stern, Stein, and Bloom (1956) and by the second experimental design used by Holt and Luborsky (1958). The emphasis in these studies was to limit assessment ratings to the particular criterion or set of criteria involved. In the Stern, Stein, and Bloom analytic studies no specific intervening variables existed although a common conceptual framework was used to organize the discussion of results. An assessment model was clearly and unequivocally set up on the basis of the criteria of the roles required by the situation for which behavior was to be predicted. The framework mentioned above consists of eight categories, listed under three main headings: (1) interpersonal relations (involving behavior reaction to others and coping mechanisms); (2) inner state (under which are included impulse-acceptance, impulse-control, and energy level); (3) goal orientation (with sub-ratings on autonomous-homonomous balance, self-maintenance, and organization and integration). This list of needs and their definitions was based largely on Murray's work.

Assessment in Stern, Stein, and Bloom's view is equally concerned with evaluation of personality and a thorough understanding of the environment in which the assessed individual is to act. Furthermore, basic to assessment methodology was the study of the congruence between data obtained from the analysis of the individual and the characteristics of the hypothetical model. Subsequently, refinements were instituted for the purpose of cross validation. Employing this "analytic" method, the assessors arrived at a judgment of congruence through staff conferences. In analytic methodology, as well as in the three others used by them (empirical, synthetic, and configurational), the authors employed the theoretical proposition that behavior is a function of the transactional relationship between the person and his environment. Such an approach to predictive assessment seems a most meaningful one; the combination of a theoretical framework and of thoroughly evaluated criteria has led to high validities for the predictions in their work.

Holt and Luborsky's research (1958) on the selection of psychiatric residents at the Menninger School of Psychiatry began in an organized fashion a year after the Kelly and Fiske study of clinical psychologists, and was brought to fruition after ten years of labor. They discontinued the first experimental design, which involved hundreds of ratings, test scores, supervisors' evaluations, interviewers' impressions, etc.; and a second, more sophisticated design was devised, emphasizing the intensive rather than extensive approach, and concentrating on a few techniques to gain maximum understanding. These included a thorough job analysis, evaluation of good and poor residents, and the development of a list of 32 variables on which each subject was to be rated. Each of the 32 items was described in some detail; they fell into the following major categories: motivation for psychiatric work, self-orientation, orientation towards others, social adjustment, handling of emotions, intellectual effectiveness, honesty, and pathological tendencies. The value of these rating scales for their study cannot be underestimated, since they served to focus upon desirable and undesirable aspects of personality in the residents. However, they were not designed to provide a comprehensive set of categories for describing personality, and bear only upon such personal qualities as were thought necessary for psychiatric work. Like the Stern, Stein, and Bloom ratings, they were limited to particular criteria, in this case the choice of physicians likely to become good psychiatrists.

The instrument for assessment described in the following pages was developed with the aim of comprehending individual personality rather than for specific prediction purposes. In what follows, we present a comprehensive theoretical system of character dimensions which should encompass a broad range of individual styles, resources, weaknesses, and attributes. The theoretically derived dimensions are then incorporated into specifically defined categories, expressed as rating scales. A complete set of ratings of the data obtained from and about an individual should serve as a relatively complete description of the characterological aspects of that particular person. A review of the psychoanalytic theory of character will lead into the discussion of our assessment scheme.[1]

---

[1] After completion of the development of our assessment scheme as well as the writing of this book an extensive outline of assessment variables similar in several respects to ours, and also based on psychoanalytic theory, was published by Grete L. Bibring, *et al.*, in "A Study of the Psychological Processes in Pregnancy and of the Earliest Mother-Child Relationship. II. Methodological Considerations," *The Psychoanalytic Study of the Child*, 1961, *16*: 25–72. Besides definitions of other variables this outline contains a particularly detailed and useful Glossary of Defenses. No rating scales or other forms of quantification are reported.

# 2
# PSYCHOANALYTIC CONCEPTIONS
# OF CHARACTER

For any systematic organization of data leading to the assessment of character, a theory of some kind is necessary. The present writers, as mentioned above, chose psychoanalytic theory for the framework of their research. A special difficulty exists, however, in regard to psychoanalytic theory in general and its conceptions of "character" in particular. Psychoanalytic conceptions of character have changed from time to time as psychoanalytic theory developed. This is also true of other psychoanalytic concepts; they have been revised, amplified, modified, or discarded as time went on. Unfortunately, there is no final and complete statement of the theory. The *Outline of Psychoanalysis* (1938), one of Freud's last works, is quite general, abstract, and sweeping: it neither defines all the major psychoanalytic concepts nor their relationships with each other; and one may say that to some extent Rapaport's *The Structure of Psychoanalytic Theory* (1960) also talks about the theory more than it defines or states it. Lacking an authoritative statement in which formulations and definitions of all concepts are brought up-to-date, and in which the relationships between concepts are defined, an investigator is forced to review the concepts he works with and indicate to his readers exactly how he uses them. In the paragraphs following we shall attempt a short review of the psychoanalytic conceptions of "character" and establish a working definition for the purposes of psychological assessment.

*11*

Freud seems to mention the term "character" for the first time in *The Interpretation of Dreams* (1900): "What we describe as our 'character' is based on the memory traces of our impressions; and, moreover, the impressions which have had the greatest effect on us—those of our earliest youth—are precisely the ones which scarcely ever become conscious." This statement seems to be a forerunner of a structural conception of character.

A much more extensive foundation was laid for the psychoanalytic study of character by Freud's investigations of the libidinal drives. In *Three Essays on the Theory of Sexuality* (1905) he describes the now well-known phases of libidinal development. These are closely related to various body zones, all of which center around apertures of the body. In very early childhood the strongest opportunities for sexual pleasure (pleasure, that is, which goes beyond the stilling of hunger) reside in the region of the mouth; somewhat later the eliminative body zones move into the foreground as areas in which pleasure may be experienced; while later and finally the zones of the sexual organs become important. From this Freud developed his conception of the oral, anal and phallic-genital phases of the libidinal drives. Further analytic work by Freud himself and by others later showed that while all people develop through these stages, they go through them in somewhat different ways and may retain needs for oral or anal satisfactions later in life; some may attain a genital level of development (psychologically speaking) only to a degree, lesser or greater as the case may be. Freud came to the conclusion that the relationship of the person to his environment, and particularly towards other people, varies according to his level of libidinal development. However, not only the predominance of particular libidinal drives determines a person's orientation, but also the person's internal reaction to his own drives. After discussing *sublimation* and *reaction formation,* two modes in which the individual reacts to his own drive, Freud states: "What we describe as a person's 'character' is built up to a considerable extent from the material of sexual excitations and is composed of instincts that have been fixed since childhood, of constructions achieved by means of sublimation, and of other constructions, employed for effectively holding in check perverse impulses which have been recognized as being unutilizable. The multifariously perverse sexual disposition of childhood can accordingly be regarded as the source of a number of our virtues, in so far as through reaction-formation it stimulates their development." (Freud, 1905, p. 238–9.)

The best known and perhaps most important single contribution which Freud made to characterology is his paper on "Character and Anal Erotism" (1908) where he reports primarily an empirical finding. He had observed that in people with prominent character traits of orderliness, parsimony, and obstinacy there regularly turns out to be also a preponderance of concerns with the anal region and with the feelings and circumstances surrounding defecation. After discussing this type of character in some detail, Freud provides a stimulus for other investigators: "One ought to consider whether other types of character do not also show a connection with the excitability of particular erotogenic zones. As yet, I am aware only of the intense, 'burning' ambition of those who formerly suffered from enuresis. At any rate one can give a formula for the formation of the ultimate character from the constituent character-traits: the permanent character traits are either unchanged perpetuations of the original impulses, sublimations of them, or reaction formations against them." (Freud, 1908, p. 50.) It seems likely that Abraham's contributions in particular, which will be discussed below, were in part stimulated by this suggestion of Freud.

Freud himself, however, never seemed to make any systematic attempt at formulating an exhaustive listing of character variations. In various writings he used his findings concerning the anal character for purposes of illustration or general documentation. In "The Excretory Functions in Psychoanalysis and Folklore" (1913a) Freud mentions the displacement, under the influence of repression, of interest in excrement onto money, and he says: "Important constituents in the formation of character are developed, or strengthened, from the repression of coprophilic desires." (Freud, 1913a, p. 90.) In "The Predisposition to Obsessional Neurosis" (1913b), Freud attempts to differentiate between the fate of an instinct in neurosis and in character development. There he writes: "In the sphere of character-development we again meet with the same instinctual forces whose workings we have already discovered in the neuroses. . . . In the formation of character either repression is not at work at all or it easily attains its aim, which is to replace the repressed impulses by reaction formations and sublimations. . . ." (Freud, 1913b, p. 129.) This seems to stress the relative absence of conflict in character development as opposed to the state of affairs in neurosis.

The concept of character appears in a somewhat new and different light in Freud's paper on "Some Character-Types met with in Psychoanalytic Work" (1915). Foreshadowing Wilhelm Reich's views on character defenses, Freud writes: "When the physician is carrying out psychoanalytic treatment of a neurotic, his interest is by no means primarily directed to the patient's character. He is far more desirous to know what the symptoms signify, what instinctual impulses lurk behind them and are satisfied by them, and by what transitions the mysterious path has led from those impulses to these symptoms. But the technique which he is obliged to follow soon constrains him to direct his immediate curiosity towards other objectives. He observes that his investigation is threatened by resistances set up against him by the patient, and these resistances he may justly attribute to the latter's character, which now acquires the first claim on his interest.

"What opposes itself to the physician's labors is not always those traits of character which the patient recognizes in himself and which are attributed to him by those around him. Peculiarities in the patient which he had seemed to possess only in a modest degree are often displayed in surprising intensity, or attitudes reveal themselves in him which in other relations of life would not have been betrayed." (Freud, 1915, p. 318.) The "types" of character which Freud mentions in this paper are, however, not immediately referable to specific drive or defense issues in the usual sense; they are "the exceptions," "those wrecked by success," and those showing "criminality from a sense of guilt." An entire orientation towards life based on drives, on defenses, and on particular life experiences, formed the character described by Freud in these cases which manifested itself as a complicated resistance in analysis.

A preliminary introduction of the concept of ego (not yet in its technical, structural sense) as an element in character formation is found in the short paper, "On the Transformation of

Instincts with Special Reference to Anal-Erotism" (1916). Freud speaks about the character traits of orderliness, parsimony, and obstinacy in a person as ". . . modes of reaction specially favored by his ego which had been established during his development in the course of the absorption of his anal-erotism." (Freud, 1916, p. 164.)

During his lifetime Freud often attempted theoretical formulations in various directions. One such attempt, relevant to our discussion of character, is found in his paper on "Libidinal Types" (1931). Here he is concerned with an attempt at reducing the "infinite variety" of "general features of humanity" to a limited number of types. We must remember that by 1931 Freud had already introduced his structural theory, in which the entire mental apparatus is defined by the three institutions of id, ego, and superego. Thus, in "Libidinal Types" he can argue that ". . . . there is no need to suppose that, even in the psychical sphere, these libidinal types are the only possible ones; if we take other characteristics as our basis of classification we might be able to distinguish a whole series of other psychological types (Freud, 1931, p. 247). He argues that types should be formulated as normal variations. They should not primarily be defined by clinical pictures. "In their extreme developments, however, they may well approximate to clinical pictures and so help to bridge the gulf which is assumed to exist between the normal and the pathological." (Ibid., p. 248.) He then describes three types: The erotic, the narcissistic, and the obsessional. The criterion for each of these types is the primary locus of concentration of the libido. If it is primarily in the id, we have the erotic type; the obsessional type is thus related to the superego, and the narcissistic type to the ego, with the aim of self-preservation. This theory may be described as triangular, and there are three possible mixed types. "The ideal norm" would be a fairly even combination of all three. Applying this system to pathology, Freud postulates a relationship between the erotic type and hysteria, the obsessional type and obsessive neurosis, and the narcissistic type and psychosis. He adds, however, that: "Experience testifies that persons of all these types can live free from neurosis. The pure types marked by the undisputed predominance of a single psychical agency seem to have a better prospect of manifesting themselves as pure character formations. . . ." (*Ibid.*, p. 250.)

There seems to be little doubt possible that Freud in this classification oversimplified things greatly. It was an interesting attempt to combine structural, dynamic, and economic considerations which might be relevant to a classification of character types. Freud himself did not follow up these conceptions in any subsequent writings; nor have any other investigators. This triangular classification neglects qualitative differences introduced into character formation by the relative predominance of varying factors in the ego; it does injustice to the complexity of possible sources of character development.

While the preceding quotations summarize fairly completely Freud's *explicit* statements concerning character, statements he himself never did summarize in any conclusive manner, we must mention some of his other contributions which are *implicitly* of much greater importance for the theory of character. Outstanding among them is his discovery and description of the processes of identification (cf. "Mourning and Melancholia" [1917a]). We shall not recapitulate the metapsychology of identification here; it is enough to say that this mechanism provides the most important single vehicle by means of which a person, particularly the growing child, models himself on others and acquires the characteristics of others for his own behavioral repertoire. Processes of identification lead to results in various regions of the mental apparatus. They contribute to the development of the ego, and most importantly to the development of the superego.

A decisive conceptualization relevant to the theory of character is, of course, Freud's systematization of the concept of the ego in *The Ego and the Id* (1923) where he defines the ego as "a coherent organization of mental processes" which comes about as the result of environmentally caused modifications of the id. At the same time, the ego is described as the main organ for the regulation of adaptive processes. Furthermore, since development of the ego is conceived to be dependent to a high degree on experience, and experience is different for each growing individual, we must assume that differences in ego content and ego structure account for a considerable variety of individual differences. Thus, the ego becomes the main carrier of individual

character features although features of the superego as well as of the id contribute to this variety. We will see below that Fenichel considers his own definition of character as nearly identical with that of the ego.

In *The Ego and the Id* Freud, besides conceptualizing the ego generally, also makes some specific contributions to the understanding of "character," which here is thought of in terms of the individual qualities of a person's ego. He refers to the previously mentioned processes of identification by means of which external objects (such as the representations of other people) are taken into the ego when cathexis is withdrawn from them. More precisely, the representations of the external object become a part of the general store of integrated experience registered in memory after an object loss, that is, after the external object may have disappeared in external reality, perhaps due to abandonment or death, or when it may have been given up as an important external object by the person's ego. Then ". . . an object-cathexis has been replaced by an identification . . . this kind of substitution has a great share in determining the form taken by the ego and . . . it makes an essential contribution towards building up what is called its 'character.'" (Freud, 1923, p. 28.) Speaking further about the role of identification processes, particularly in the context of the giving up of objects, Freud says that ". . . the process, especially in the early phases of development, is a very frequent one, and it makes it possible to suppose that the character of the ego is a precipitate of abandoned object-cathexes and that it contains the history of those object-choices." (*Ibid.*, p. 29.)

Processes of identification lead also to the institution of the superego. While we will not review Freud's gradually developing formulations concerning the ego-ideal and superego, we may state generally that the contents of the superego, derived from the growing child's perceptions of the characteristics of the parent figures, also contribute necessarily to the qualities and thus to the "character" of his ego. Another source of variability between people in addition to the contents of the superego can be found in the various degrees of strength and demandingness of individual superegos, as well as in the different degrees of integration or opposition between the ego and superego of different individuals. The more detailed relations between identifications

which are constituent parts of the ego and those which are primarily parts of the superego cannot be discussed here; our purpose at this point is merely to emphasize the important parts both of these play in the formation of character.

Other investigators began to be interested in problems of character and, especially in the beginning, followed Freud's general approach of studying character features as they derive from the vicissitudes of libidinal development. Relevant here are the contributions of Sadger (1910) and of Jones (1918), both concerning elaborations of the theory of the anal character. Of special importance, however, are the writings of Abraham (1921, 1924, and 1925). In the first of these papers he presents a wealth of clinical observations in elaborating Freud's and Jones's earlier descriptions of the anal character. He particularly traces the derivation of certain characterological traits from the retentive and the eliminative modes of the anal phase, and from the narcissistic injury children may suffer during the period of toilet training. He cites especially the traits of cleanliness, of orderliness, of pleasure in production and in achievement, of a special tendency towards obedience and yielding to others as opposed to a sense of power, of being able to do things, and of insisting on doing them in one's own way. He discusses the need of anal characters for maintaining an exaggerated sense of autonomy and their resentments of any limitations of their power. He illustrates how anally oriented people often find it difficult to give things away, to make presents, and to pay money. All these trends may be interwoven with desires to control others and make them dependent. Abraham finds differences between the productivity of the anal character and the productivity characteristic of people who have come closer to the genital level of development. The anal characters often emphasize the processes and means of production over the actual object to be produced. There are tendencies of procrastination, as well as predilections for drawing up timetables, production schedules, rules and procedures, all of which interfere with actual productivity. The more the latter is hindered and inhibited, an interest in possessions increases which also is overdetermined by a turning away from real objects. Thus, interests in accumulating and holding property, for instance, may be pursued at the expense of interpersonal relationships. Concern

with possessions may take, among other things, also the form of a desire to invest only in things of permanent value and to avoid the pursuit of transitory pleasures or gains. Abraham refers to Jones's descriptions of the tendency of anal people to collect objects and he emphasizes their inclination to hoard even worthless or useless things. The desire to save may also extend to the saving of time; Abraham describes a variety of ways in which such people go about saving time, often very unproductively. He concludes by describing the tendency towards negativism and contradiction, or opposition for its own sake, frequently found in anal characters. At the end of this paper, which is one of the richest of all the psychoanalytic writings on character, Abraham emphasizes his desire to draw attention to the characterological derivatives of the pregenital phases of the libido. He thus prepares the ground for investigation of characterological and psychopathological derivatives of the oral phase which is accomplished in the next paper to be discussed (Abraham, 1924).

He begins with a few important theoretical observations. He finds that those elements of infantile sexuality which are excluded from participation in the sexual life of the adult, are particularly important for character formation. Thus character traits may represent elaborations of partial libidinal drives which cannot find direct and immediate expression and gratification in the adult. One consequence of this, according to Abraham, is the smaller variety of oral than of anal character traits, since there is less need to modify the libidinal cathexes of the mouth and oral zone, many of which can still be utilized in adult life. He stresses the close developmental interaction of orality and anality. The end of weaning and the beginning of toilet training, for instance, often overlap in time and this may reinforce tendencies towards displacement of concerns from one area to the other.

Abraham follows the implications of more subtle features of libidinal development, especially of the two stages of passive taking-in and of aggressive biting, in much detail. Each of these stages may lead to quite different characterological derivatives, depending in part upon degrees and kinds of gratifications or deprivation. Thus he finds that overindulgence during the receptive phase may lead to the character traits of imperturbable optimism, of passivity grounded in a belief that somebody will

always take care of one, but also of generosity (via an identification with the bounteous mother), and of sociability and openness to new ideas and to life in general. Deprivation during the receptive phase is likely to give rise to later craving for objects, avarice, a fear of losing what one has, and a tendency to hoard, as well as general pessimism and a striving for security. From the biting, orally sadistic phase which coincides with the appearance of teeth, may derive trends of aggressive demandingness, and of impatience; exploitativeness, hostility, dislike of other people, and envy might be further manifestations. Greater complexities stem from the interactions of traits. Oral and anal issues may interplay in the areas of intake and retention of matter; oral implications of giving may become interrelated with derivatives of the mode of elimination, and so forth.

Through his exhaustive treatment of pregenital contributions to character development, Abraham paves the way for his discussion of the genital character. Again, he begins with some theoretical considerations including a short, admittedly incomplete, definition of a person's character: It is ". . . the sum of his instinctive reactions towards his social environment." (Abraham, 1925, p. 408.) He sees a sharp distinction between the psychoanalytic conception of character and the (then) prevailing conception of character as a permanent and relatively ingrained pattern due mostly to heredity and early upbringing. Repeatedly, he emphasizes the changeable nature of character and supports this by pointing to the interplay between regressive and progressive developments during a lifetime, and to the fact of ambivalence which makes a person swing from one form of a character trait to its very opposite.

The genital character emerges as the result of two processes. One consists of the gradual elimination of derivatives of more primitive stages, the other of the overcoming of the Oedipus complex and particularly of the narcissistic and hostile impulses and affects inherent in it. Abraham describes few specific characteristics of the genital character. He mainly mentions traits of friendliness and a generally well-wishing attitude toward close persons and the community in general. Almost more important are the integrative aspects of genital character formation. In this last, most mature stage of characterological development, achieve-

ments from earlier stages are synthesized: the oral traits of enterprise and energy, anal traits of endurance and perseverance, and strength for the struggle of existence deriving from the sadistic stage. One of the most important characteristics of the genital character is balance and proportion; excessive ambivalence and oscillation between different modes are checked and prevented and derivatives from earlier libidinal stages are hindered from interfering with mature object relations. The maturity of object relations is characterized primarily by the ability to love some object, such as another person, as a whole. When the castration complex and the oedipal ties have been overcome, fears that were previously experienced in relationship to certain parts of the object are eliminated and positive, friendly feelings can then be experienced toward the entire object. Fewer specific traits are enumerated for the genital character than were given for the anal and the oral in the preceding papers; this seems to be the case because it is impossible to trace the genital character to any particular distinct libidinal component or mode. Integration, many-sidedness, avoidance of excess, and the capacity fully to love an object are the important features of the genital character as formulated by Abraham.

Up to this point in the history of psychoanalysis the conceptions of character and its development are based primarily on the genetic relationships between certain character traits and the libidinal stages and modes. There is some emphasis on the effects of repression which is the main factor interfering with direct gratification of various partial drives. The influence of a variety of types of ego-defense upon character formation becomes an issue treated in great detail by the next writer to be discussed. The work of Wilhelm Reich, however, was anticipated by Abraham who in 1925 stated that clinical psychoanalysis must often deal with pathological deformities of character. All along, Abraham stressed the difficulty of character analysis, but emphasized its rewarding nature.

Reich's several and important contributions, summarized in his book *Character Analysis* (1949), to the psychoanalytic investigation of character structure fall into the years after Freud had published *The Ego and the Id*. In his writings the emphasis shifts from the study of the libidinal roots of the character formation to the defensive functions of the character structure. However, Reich (before he entered upon his adventures with the concept of the Orgone) does not by any means abandon the recognition of the importance of the libidinal phases and of their derivatives for character development; on the contrary, he repeatedly allies himself with Freud and attacks the "deviationists." He takes the findings of Freud, Abraham, and Jones concerning the oral, anal, phallic, and genital characters for granted, although he makes further contributions to their description. It is interesting to note that Reich, who subscribed strongly to certain basic marxist ideas which he at times superimposed rather forcedly upon his psychoanalytic formulations, nevertheless introduces a specific form of what, in later phases of psychoanalytic theorizing, becomes the psychosocial point of view.

Reich's theory of character development is essentially as follows: He assumes that at any time when, due to external factors and particularly to the repressive intervention of parental figures, anxiety over sexual, partial drives is aroused, the child masters this "infantile phobia" by turning some of these very drives to defensive purposes. At the same time there occurs an identification with the repressive and inhibiting aspects of the parental figure. Regressive reactivations of earlier libidinal issues also may occur and their energies and modes then may participate in the development of the defensively functioning character. The period during which the solution of the Oedipus complex is attempted is considered especially important for the development of character features.

Dynamically and economically character structure is considered by Reich as being quite analogous to a neurotic symptom. Just like a symptom, character contains both the defensive and the impulse-aspects of an intrapsychic conflict. Reich writes: "Character formation begins as a definite form of the solution of the Oedipus complex. The conditions which lead to this particular form of the solution of conflicts are specific for character formation. (These conditions correspond to the social conditions of today and their influence on infantile sexuality. With the change of these social conditions, the conditions of character formation will also change, and with that, the character structures.)" (Reich, 1949, p. 146.) Character, however, is more extensive than a symptom. It represents a consolidated defensive organization which becomes habitual and rigid. It implies a "chronic alteration of the ego" which often serves as a defensive "armor."

In *Character-Analysis* Reich introduces his discussion of character structure by emphasizing the importance of its understanding for therapeutic reasons. He points out the necessity of analyzing the patient's characterological traits and attitudes prior to analyzing the infantile, sexual conflict. He insists that the results of analyzing the infantile, sexual material are bound to be short-lived as long as there are still unanalyzed characterological defenses which can be reinstituted against them. This train of reasoning has lastingly influenced psychoanalytic technique. It clearly is expressed, for instance, in Freud's argument against attempts to shorten psychoanalytic treatment by going right to the center of the infantile neurosis. Freud makes the analogy of firemen going into a burning house to right the upset oil lamp which had started the fire. (Freud, 1937.)

From the various kinds of character symptoms and traits Reich especially singles out the *formal* aspects of a patient's behavior. Among them he discusses posture, manner of speech, movement, appearance, and demeanor. Motility, with its basic possibilities for serving the expression and discharge of sexual impulses, and the defensive inhibitions of motility are central to his interest. Thus he focuses considerably on the bodily, physical aspects of the character armor. The physical reification of conceptions of psychic energy (in terms of motility and muscular rigidity) provides very likely the link between Reich's highly creative, early psychoanalytic thinking and his later fantastic preoccupation with "bio-physical," orgone energies.

Reich discusses a number of character types in considerable detail. He expands the catalogue begun by Freud, Abraham, Jones, and others. There is the hysterical, the compulsive, the phallic-narcissistic, the passive-feminine, the paranoid-aggressive, the sadistic, and the masochistic character in addition to various other types defined by more individual themes, such as an "aristocratic" character.

He describes various typical configurations of traits in different kinds of character. The following abbreviated descriptions represent some of the more important character types:

*Hysterical Character.* This type usually shows a clearly sexual quality in its general behavior in the form of coquetry and provocativeness; body movements are agile, soft, and rolling; there is some general apprehensiveness, some excitability, a general inconstancy of reactions as well as some suggestibility. The sexual quality of behavior, however, does not imply genuine sexual interest but is designed to test the responsiveness of others which is basically dreaded.

*Compulsive Character.* In this type we find a general, pedantic concern for orderliness, circumstantial, ruminative thinking, thriftiness, avarice, and a tendency to collect things. There is indecision, doubt, and distrust as well as restraint, control, and a blockedness of affect. Reactions of sympathy (as a reaction formation against unconscious sadistic trends) and guilt feelings are also common.

*Phallic-narcissistic Character.* This group is marked by self-confidence, arrogance, elasticity, and vigorousness in general behavior, impressiveness, haughtiness, vanity, dignity, superiority, aggressive courage, and high erective potency with, however, little orgastic satisfaction.

*Masochistic Character.* There is a dominant sensation of suffering, a tendency to complain, an inclination towards damaging the self, self-depreciation, a compulsion to torture others, and an awkward, atactic manner of moving.

Since the quality and the form of character development, according to Reich, are in part determined by the nature of the libidinal drives against which the ego attempts to consolidate a defense, there is a correlation between character types and libidinal stages. Thus depressive traits are coordinated with orality; masochistic, and genital-narcissistic traits with the phallic level; hysterical traits with the genital-incestuous phase; and compulsive ones with a sadistic-anal fixation.

As for Freud and the other psychoanalytic writers, reaching genitality represents the optimal libidinal development of a person; also for Reich. His description of the genital character, however, is, just as Abraham's, mostly in terms of what that form of character excludes. In part, this fact is accounted for by the at least partial definition of the other character types in terms of traits deriving from inhibitions, fixations, restrictions, and defenses against sexual drives. The genital character, on the other hand, is by definition largely free of all these inhibitory restrictions. However, some positively stated characteristics include those of pliability, flexibility, adaptability, a lack of extreme reactions, an ability to experience full sexual gratification in orgasm as well as to give oneself and of oneself without fear of loss or dissolution. Also there should be solidly established self-confidence, rationality, and a relative lack of neurotic guilt feelings.

In this short review of Reich's contributions we concentrated upon his descriptions of the characterological types and neglected to do justice to the extensive and thorough genetic interpretations which are to be found in his writings. His work, disregarding its later elaborations in terms of the orgone, remains to this day a fundamental contribution to psychoanalytic characterology.

Anna Freud's contributions to the understanding of ego defenses (A. Freud, 1936) represent an important step in the development of ego psychology and thus are relevant to the theory of character. Particularly they pave the way for Fenichel's formulations concerning character disorders (Fenichel, 1945). Anna Freud reviews briefly the historical development of the concept of "defense" and summarizes the various forms of ego defense described in the psychoanalytic literature, especially in her father's works. She presents a list of mechanisms which includes regression, repression, reaction-formation, isolation, undoing, projection, introjection, turning against the self, reversal, and sublimation. In addition, she introduces denial, identification with the aggressor, and intellectualization. All of these serve the "protection of the ego against instinctual demands." Quoting S. Freud in *Inhibitions, Symptoms, and Anxiety* (Freud, 1926), she refers to the "intimate connection between special forms of defense and particular illnesses," and she furthermore discusses the possibility of certain correlations between phases of early development and the appearance and prominent use of certain defense mechanisms. Without going into the details of these discussions we may nevertheless note that the defenses are assumed to play a rather central role in the total functioning of the ego and we may thus expect them to influence significantly the style and quality of the functioning of a particular, individual ego.

Anna Freud says little about character as such. She refers briefly to Reich's conceptions of character armor, emphasizing especially its manifestations in motility and posture. She speaks about the "residues of very vigorous defensive processes in the past" which have developed into "permanent character traits" but returns then to a discussion of broader issues in relation to the analysis of ego resistances and defenses.

Fenichel (1945) presents the most complete and exhaustive summary available of the psychoanalytic theory of character. He considers the study of character as an integral part of "ego psychology." The interest of psychoanalysts in the investigation of character phenomena is explained by him as due to the necessity of analyzing resistances and defenses but also by the increased frequency of patients with character disorders who apply for psychoanalytic treatment. This fact he describes as at least partly due to general changes in social conditions and he discusses briefly some possible relations between societal structures and the development of particular character traits. Reich, as was mentioned above, had followed some similar thoughts although from a socialistic point of view. Fenichel, in defining "character," emphasizes that its formation is determined by a wider range of factors than merely those of defensive mechanisms. The particular way in which prominent instinctual demands are channeled and expressed is of at least equal importance, but decisive is the overall, habitual, dynamic organization in which the ego simultaneously deals with the multiple demands of the id, the superego, of external reality, and which is influenced by the ego's defensive and adaptive resources. Fenichel utilizes Waelder's conception of "multiple function" (Waelder, 1936) to account for the ego's tendency to deal with all these forces in an integrated manner. Clearly implied here is also the concept of ego synthesis (Nunberg, 1931). Fenichel's definition of character reflects all of these conceptualizations: "Character, as the habitual mode of bringing into harmony the tasks presented by internal demands and by the external world, is necessarily a function of the constant, organized, and integrating part of the personality which is the ego; . . . The question of character would thus be the question of when and how the ego acquires the qualities by

which it habitually adjusts itself to the demands of instinctual
drives and of the external world, and later also of the superego."

Essentially following Freud's earlier thinking about the genesis
of character traits as reviewed above (Freud, 1908), Fenichel
classifies them into two major groups: those traits that serve the
discharge of an impulse ("sublimation type") and those which
serve the suppression of an impulse ("reactive type"). His description of types falling into the first of these categories is unfortunately brief. Fenichel rightly emphasizes our general lack
of knowledge concerning the "successful" mechanisms by means
of which the ego habitually serves the discharge and gratification
of various instinctual demands; he adds what would appear to
be a theoretical statement of great consequence, namely that
". . . it is probable that all sublimation is performed by mechanisms identical with or similar to identification." It is quite possible that the potential variety of character traits which can be
acquired through processes of identification is much greater than
that of traits arising from the interaction between ego defenses
and typical instinctual demands. Perhaps it is due to this great
variety that no typically recurrent classes of sublimation-type
traits have so far become obvious.

The reactive character traits are further subdivided by
Fenichel into several groups. There are those which imply "pathological behavior toward the id" and which include frigid, phobic,
and counterphobic types as well as those involving "identification
with the aggressor." Other forms include habitual tendencies of
the ego to rationalize and idealize instinctual impulses. Other
forms of reactive character development are represented in the
already well-known forms of oral, anal, urethral, phallic, and
genital orientations. Under the heading of "Pathological behavior
toward the superego," Fenichel deals with the various ways in
which the ego may habitually deal with strong feelings of guilt;
they include tendencies to atone, to punish or be punished, or to
suffer remorse. Typical defenses which come into play in relation
to the superego are those of projection, introjection, or rebellion,
and acting-out. Moral masochism, certain forms of achievement
striving, as well as some kinds of criminality also fall into this
group. Finally, Fenichel reviews certain manifestations of "Pathological behavior towards external objects."

There is obviously a great profusion of various characterological forms. This profusion on one hand does justice to the variety of possible developments but it also makes classification difficult. In a final section of his chapter, Fenichel returns to the problem of classifying character types, attempting their division by analogy to the general divisions of neuroses. He finds justification for this in ". . . the simple reason that mechanisms similar to the various forms of symptom formations are likewise operative in the formation of character traits." Thus he establishes a continuity between neurotic (including psychotic) and characterological developments and formulates the classes of phobic and hysterical characters, compulsive, cyclic, and schizoid characters. In general it appears that Fenichel's approach to the genetic explanation of various forms of character development as well as his attempts at classifying them, which follows closely the thinking of Freud and Reich although he elaborates on it, is generally accepted in psychoanalytic theory today. There are further contributions to the description and genetic and dynamic explanation of certain character types such as the one by Michaels of the impulsive character (Michaels, 1958) but they will not be further reviewed here.

Fenichel emphasizes the closeness of his definition of "character" to the psychoanalytic definition of the "ego." Character as the "habitual mode of bringing into harmony the tasks presented by internal demands and by the external world," is clearly another way of formulating the ego's adaptive, defensive, and synthetic efforts. The psychoanalytic formulations of the nature of character reviewed so far stem primarily from the clinical and therapeutic phases of psychoanalysis. As the psychology of the ego was developed and expanded, however, more and more observations of facts as well as theory concerning the ego's functioning became available. With that, the theoretical emphasis shifts somewhat to the study of the developmental and the adaptive aspects of the ego, of its resources, the conditions under which it matures, and on the circumstances which influence its contents and the quality of its reactions. All of this, then, is clearly also relevant to the psychoanalytic conception of character structure. A brief review of some of the major issues in ego psychology is, therefore, necessary.

In one of his late papers, Freud reviews the influence of defensive struggles in childhood upon ego development and comes to the conclusion that not all the individual differences in ego structure can be accounted for by experience and as the result of the ego's interaction with the environment (Freud, 1937). He states on the contrary, that: "We have no reason to dispute the existence and importance of primary congenital variations in the ego." One suggestive observation in that direction, according to Freud, is that each individual "selects only *certain* of the possible defensive mechanisms. . . ." He thinks ". . . that, even before the ego exists, its subsequent lines of development, tendencies and reactions are already determined."

This line of thinking is developed further in some of the ego-psychological writings, especially those of Hartmann (1939, 1950). He conceives of a number of apparatuses, which form the necessary basic equipment for the development of adaptive behavior, and which rest on "constitutional givens." He says: "These components of *ego constitution* deserve our attention just as much as the components of drive constitution" (1939, p. 101). Examples of such apparatuses are those which mature into functions such as perception, motility, memory, intelligence, etc. It becomes an important postulate in ego psychology that these apparatuses and functions, although they may become involved in intrapsychic conflicts sooner or later, do not depend on such conflicts for their development. They are considered to constitute the so-called "conflict-free ego sphere" and are thus distinguished from, for instance, an obsessive character trait such as stinginess which depends for its development on certain conflicts over anal retention and elimination. While the developmental study of the various ego apparatuses and functions is still incomplete (although researches such as those of Werner and Piaget have relevance), it is clear that the relative maturation and refinement of these various functions at any given developmental stage must influence the growth of the ego as well as its resourcefulness in its tasks of mediation and adaptation. Even the choice of certain defense mechanisms, or the relatively greater utilization of one as compared to another, may to a degree be affected by the development of adaptive ego functions in the conflict-free sphere. It may, for instance, be more probable that a basically highly intelligent person comes to rely on the defense of intellectualization than a person with limited endowment. It becomes clear from these considerations that a full description of a given person's character structure at any given time would have to include statements concerning his adaptive resources and strengths, both in their extent and in their particular individual quality, since they surely affect the person's "habitual mode" of functioning.

An issue raised already by Hartmann and later discussed in much more detail by Rapaport (1951, 1958) is that of the ego's autonomy. The fact that certain apparatuses—essential for the ego's adaptive functioning and including those apparatuses such as memory, motility, perception, discharge thresholds, and others, do not depend on psychic conflict for their development—is described by attributing "primary autonomy" to them. Their development is considered as due to maturational processes which, to be sure, are thought to interact with the impact of experience and possibly with various intrapsychic conflicts later on. These primary autonomous ego factors are conceptualized as independent developmental roots of the ego (cf. also Hartmann, Kris, and Loewenstein, 1946). At later developmental stages this primary autonomy of the ego is supplemented by functions which gain secondary autonomy. Not only various functions but also certain structures and apparatuses which derive originally from expressions of drives, or from manifestations of defensive efforts, or as the result of the interaction of both, may, in the course of time undergo a "change of function," become relatively independent from the id, and may become part of the ego's adaptive organizations. Character traits as described by Reich and Fenichel, which have become relatively permanent institutions in the ego and through which the ego accomplishes part of its adaptive tasks, may be examples of such secondarily autonomous aspects of the ego. The development of structures and functions having secondary autonomy is, of course, one of the major aims of education.

The idea of the at least partial determination of individual character structure by the society in which a child grows up, already encountered in Reich's and Fenichel's writings, is observationally tested, studied in its relation to libidinal development, and put into the general context of psychoanalytic ego psychology by Erikson (1950, 1959). He investigates especially the lasting contributions to the development of the individual ego which result from the interplay between parental (and thus indirectly societal) influences and demands, and the needs and capabilities of the child at any given stage of libidinal development. The child's capabilities at any given stage are studied in terms of the maturation of various apparatuses, from reflex responses to motility. From this interplay derive, at the gradual conclusion of each developmental stage, certain lasting gains that basically involve the achievement of certain fundamental orientations of the individual's ego towards the world, to other people, and towards himself. These achievements, if effected optimally, include basic trust, a basic sense and capacity for autonomy, a capability for initiative, meaningful industry, the development of a consistent sense of identity, a capacity for intimacy, for generativity, and, in later ages, a fundamental position of integrity. These "psychosocial issues" are complex, but they are solidly anchored in the libidinal stages, thus expressing instinctual needs as well as certain modalities of functioning; and they correspond at the same time to the demands and opportunities with which any society confronts the growing child at any given stage. Erikson exemplifies his thesis through observations in several cultural contexts. Clearly, the conception of "multiple functioning" referred to above, underlies all these formulations. Another basic assumption of psychoanalytic theory, namely that of the cumulativeness of libidinal development as it passes through the different stages, also underlies Erikson's approach. No later psychosocial issue can be successfully or optimally dealt with by the growing person unless the preceding issues have been reasonably well resolved. Phenomena of fixation and regression can be observed in psychosocial just as in libidinal development.

The psychosocial orientations which Erikson describes are of a somewhat different quality than are the characterological types conceptualized in earlier psychoanalytic theorizing. For one thing, Erikson's emphasis is on normal healthy development rather than on pathology. Although he is also implicitly and explicitly concerned with the effects of ego defenses, he focuses more on the adaptive elaboration and transformation of the various libidinal drives. His detailed consideration of the body zones associated with the libidinal drives, and of the physical (muscular and sensory) apparatuses which are part of these body zones, leads into his concepts of "modes." These modes (incorporation, elimination, retention, intrusion, etc.) come into play, during development, in the context of interpersonal situations, and are then elaborated into "modalities" such as "getting," "taking," "letting go," "holding on," and others. Since the theory of the libido is worked out in detail only up to adolescence, the theory of modes and modalities also is not carried into the later stages of psychosocial development. The emphasis on integration or synthesis of processes occurring in the development of the ego with the goings-on in surrounding society, including its values and ideologies, becomes more decisive in Erikson's theorizing as it concerns adolescent and postadolescent stages of development, although it is present also with regard to the earlier stages. Concerns with the processes of ego-synthesis are of particular importance in Erikson's conceptualization of the adolescent issue of identity development which refers to the consolidation, within an individual, of a workable, socially integrated character structure that incorporates all previous developmental achievements.

Although Erikson's concepts run across the dimensions of character variations discussed before, they are not irrelevant to them. Particularly in his discussions of unsuccessful solutions of the various developmental tasks he at times invokes references to the traditional categories. An unsuccessful outcome of the trust-issue, for instance, may lead to paranoid forms of development, or a fixation in the phase during which the striving for autonomy is dominant, may be part of a beginning obsessive orientation. The complexity of Erikson's categories suggests the importance of their inclusion into any system of character assessment. Judgments of the predominance of various psychosocial components, in Erikson's sense, in a given person, would cover variance due to libidinal drives, to adaptive apparatuses, and to psychosocial integrations simultaneously.

Considering the development of concepts of character from Freud's descriptions of the anal character through Erikson's formulations one is impressed by an increasing concern with complex phenomena. This concern is evident also in the recent appearance, within psychoanalysis, of the concept of the self. Various interpretations of the nature, the role, and the conceptual standing of the self have, of course, been attempted for a long time in philosophy and in academic psychology. In psychoanalytic ego psychology the self appears at first in terms of a set of self-representations (Hartmann, 1950); Jacobson (1954) adds the notion that these self-representations also become organized into a differentiated, integrated entity. Both authors relate these conceptualizations of the self to the theory of narcissism and state that it is the self rather than the ego which becomes the narcissistically cathected object. Schafer, in an unpublished paper, emphasizes that the self must be understood as a mental content rather than as a metapsychological construct of the order of ego or superego.

There can be no doubt that the contents of a person's self must have implications for his characterological functioning. This may be even more true for various formal attributes of his self. Phenomena such as self-esteem, the subjective valuation of the self, the degree of its homogeneity, the degree of its involvement with the not-self, and others, all would seem to represent significant dimensions which, in their interaction with other ego-processes, are expected to contribute to over-all adaptation. The relatively excessive valuation of the self in some narcissistic characters, or its derogation in depressions, are well-known instances. It would lead too far to attempt an integration of the various references to the self in psychoanalytic literature in this chapter. The above-mentioned instances of different valuations of the self in different clinical conditions may just suggest the relevance of certain dimensions of the self to psychoanalytic theory. But no comprehensive statement concerning the self is yet available in the literature.

Experimental work in the field of perception has in recent years been conducted increasingly in the framework of psychoanalytic theory (Klein, 1954; Gardner, Holzman, Klein, Linton, and Spence, 1959; cf. also Rapaport, 1957). Relevant for the theory of ego functioning are the consistent findings of cognitive styles typical of individual subjects. There are individually consistent ways of perceiving as well as of remembering, the consistencies manifesting themselves in the formal aspects of the perceptual or memory processes rather than in their contents. Some of these individual "cognitive styles" are conceived of by the experimenters in terms of control, thus implicitly having defensive aspects. But there is little doubt that the same characteristics can be viewed from an adaptive point of view also. They tend to dominate the manner in which a person approaches viewing the world around him (styles in viewing the self have not been specifically investigated to our knowledge), and they contribute to the forms in which stimulus material taken in becomes organized in memory or is reproduced later on (Paul, 1959). The adaptive aspect of cognitive styles, or structures, is stressed by Rapaport who states that a theory of cognition, among other things, must ". . . assume that cognitive processes create some of their components *de novo*, while others are ready-made tools available to them . . ." also, ". . . a theory of cognition must also assume that both the cognitions and the tools of cognition that emerge from cognitive processes are organized in some quasi-permanent and orderly fashion in the mind" (Rapaport, 1957, p. 158). The "tools of cognition," as opposed to the "processes" are thought of as representing structures rather than processes, the differential criterion being that structures have a much lower rate of change. Thus, cognitive styles are, in recent theorizing, found to be individual organizations with a slow rate of change, that is, a certain stability, and they influence the way in which a particular person receives, organizes, stores, and utilizes his perceptions of the world. There can be little doubt that such cognitive organizations must contribute to the habitual modes of adaptation which are stressed in definitions of character. Despite the individual forms which cognitive styles and controls may assume, it is nevertheless possible, for experimental purposes, to group subjects along some dimensions representing these styles. Dimensions used in perceptual research (within an ego-psychological orientation) include those of leveling-sharpening, focusing or scanning, constricted-flexible control, equivalence range, tolerance for unrealistic experiences, and, formulated in a somewhat different context, those of field dependence-independence (for a review of these see Gardner, *et al.*, 1959).

In our concern with cognitive styles and organizations we emphasize the formal modes through which a person's ego structures its perceptual relations to the external world. Its relations to the internal world, particularly towards the id, have so far only been encompassed in our review of various forms of defensive elaborations of drive impulses. There are instances, however, in which the ego appears to permit itself relatively undistorted perception and utilization of certain drives and fantasies, as well as modes of organizing these, all of which are not part of the ego most of the time. Under certain conditions "regressions in the service of the ego" take place; they do not imply a dangerous loss of defensive control nor do they involve a painful overwhelming of the ego's functioning by alien material. Recovery from such controlled regression does not present special difficulties to the ego, and the drives, fantasies, or affects which have entered into the compound of the ego's organizations during the period of regression contribute to the enrichment of the ego's contents and resources. The concept of "regression in the service of the ego" was introduced by Kris (1952) in the discussion of processes contributing to artistic productivity. Besides the field of (more or less original) artistic creation regression in the service of the ego comes into play in wit and humor, in empathy with others, in play, to mention just a few situations (cf. also Schafer, 1958). A person's capacity for such controlled regression has implications for the strength and flexibility of his ego functioning, for his "openness" to his own internal world, for the "richness" that can be derived from such openness and, through all these, for his adaptation particularly to his social environment. At least the degree but, ideally, also the quality of a person's capacity for such regression seems to be another important consideration in any general assessment of his character structure.

In this brief review we have seen that the psychoanalytic theory of character has come to include the individually characteristic forms of a great variety of defensive and adaptive functions, of the more or less lasting intrapsychic products of these functions, of contents deriving from individual experience, and, perhaps most of all, of the quite unique ways in which all these structures, functions, and contents become organized and come into play as an integrated unit. We have elaborated Fenichel's view that the study of character is an integral part of ego psychology. For the assessment scheme to be described below we would like to use Fenichel's definition of character as a basis: It is an individual's "habitual mode of bringing into harmony the tasks presented by internal demands and by the external world . . . (it) is necessarily a function of the constant, organized, and integrating part of the personality which is the ego. . . ." The following assessment scheme represents an effort to encompass a variety of the ego's functions, structures, and organizations in a manner which allows the description of individual nuances in all of them. It is hoped that the definitions of some of the dimensions for assessment described below may in themselves make a contribution to the psychoanalytic psychology of character.

# 3

# THE ASSESSMENT SCHEME
# AND ITS USE

The purpose of our assessment scheme is to provide a theoretically relevant, reasonably exhaustive, and conceptually consistent framework for the organization and representation of diagnostic information concerning individual character structures. The modern psychoanalytic view emphasizes the complexity of character as well as the multiplicity of its aspects. To comprehend an individual's character structure, therefore, involves more than a simple diagnostic label. Although such labels are descriptively useful, they include a good many variables about each of which we would wish to have more explicit and specific information. Thus we would desire to know about particular drive-defense configurations; about the person's particular adaptive resources and strengths; the individual styles of his cognitive functioning; his preponderant affective tones; about the level and quality of his psychosocial development; the quality and strength of his superego and the ego's relations to the superego; and about the manner in which the person views himself and which, directly or indirectly, must be expected to influence his adaptive relations. All of these aspects may be singled out for theoretical scrutiny, experimental manipulation, or for descriptive purposes in assessment. According to the principle of "multiple function" (Waelder, 1936), however, we must consider the constant interplay between and the mutual conditioning of all these aspects; they interact and co-vary in complex ways and must not be thought of as independent of one another even though we may ascribe moderate

37

and various degrees of autonomy to each one of them. This interaction between distinguishable aspects of the character can be conceptualized in terms of its being a dynamic Gestalt. Character has a certain unity; the degree of its unification being in itself an important inter-individual variable. This unity must be thought of as containing identifiable sub-units of various orders. Ultimately, it may be useful to think of hierarchies of various structures and functions in which higher-order unities include various sets of lower-order ones which in turn may overlap to different degrees. Approaches to the conceptualization and assessment of such hierarchies, however, are beyond the scope of this investigation.

The assessment scheme presented here approaches character in terms of a number of categories and dimensions. We formulated eight major categories, all of them related to ego-psychological considerations relevant to characterology. They are: A. Ideational Styles; B. Prominent Affects; C. Prominent Defenses; D. Superego; E. Adaptive Strengths; F. Sense of Self; G. Psychosocial Modalities; H. Character Elaborations. Each of these contains a number of dimensions, the definitions of which form the heads of rating scales. In formulating these categories and in setting them into their sequence, we were tempted to order them according to the history of their development in psychoanalytic theory. In that case, Prominent Defenses would probably have to occupy first place, Superego and Character Elaborations would have to follow closely, perhaps together with Prominent Affects; Adaptive Strengths and Ideational Styles would come later while Psychosocial Modalities and Sense of Self would conclude the series. For practical work with the categories, however, we found that a rough order in terms of their complexity was more useful, especially since it corresponds to the way in which the clinician makes his inferences about a person from whatever diagnostic data are available (in our study these data consist of test results and recorded interviews). Thus the order of major categories in the assessment scheme proceeds roughly from variables with relatively less complexity to variables with a greater one. This fact has further implications. The later categories in the scheme tend to include at least some of the variance represented in the earlier ones; thus, a particular Character Elaboration implies a relatively greater emphasis upon some defenses as compared to others; furthermore, some Character Elaborations imply certain Prominent Affects rather than others. Similarly, some Psychosocial Modalities have closer relations with some Adaptive Strengths than with others, and so on. The overlap of some of the categories and dimensions in the assessment scheme thus reflects the hierarchical organization of character as well as its Gestalt quality. In using the rating scales it is then not only permissible but necessary to consider ratings on the less complex variables when making ratings on the more complex ones although the latter are usually also based on additional evidence in the diagnostic data. These issues will become clearer in the discussion of the illustrative cases below.

Overlap of the scales and some correlation between the ratings on the different dimensions derive in part also from the fact that the same items of diagnostic information may contribute to ratings on several scales. All of this has to be taken into account in planning statistical treatment of assessment ratings made by using our scheme. We expect the different scales to correlate and we assume the presence of certain clusters although in the present discussion we shall refrain from stating specific hypotheses concerning the patterns of such intercorrelations.

We devised altogether 78 characterologically relevant dimensions, all of them derived from ego-psychological considerations. For each one, with two exceptions, there is a 5-point rating scale in which each step is defined. These rating scales are to be applied to whatever diagnostic data are available concerning a particular person. In our research we use clinical test data as well as transcripts of biographical interviews. It should be emphasized that especially when diagnostic information is available from tests, it is not the raw test data (scores, profiles) which form the basis for ratings. Rather, the *interpretations* of the test data provide the material to be rated. The same holds true for interview records although sometimes the content of a statement made in an interview may lead rather directly and without much transformation into the interpretation of that datum.

The assessment scheme, in principle, is independent from the nature of the available diagnostic data. In planning an assessment study it is useful, however, to plan for collecting raw data of a kind which will lend themselves to interpretation in a psychoanalytic framework. They can then be used more economically and with relatively fewer levels of inference between the data and the ratings made from them. This is one of the reasons for our using a clinical test battery consisting of WAIS, Rorschach, and TAT to provide one set of data to be rated. Rapaport, Gill, and Schafer (1945, 1946), and later Schafer (1954) have shown in much detail how these tests can be meaningfully interpreted in a psychoanalytic frame of reference. Although there are so far no equally specific and explicit approaches to the analysis of interview data, a careful outlining of the topics to be covered can elicit material maximally relevant to the dimensions in relation to which assessment is undertaken. The case discussions below will illustrate these approaches.

From these considerations we may derive several suggestions for the use of the assessment scheme:

*First,* the investigator, who ideally should have some familiarity with the psychoanalytic theory of character, should familiarize himself thoroughly not only with the eight major categories and the seventy-eight dimensions in the scheme, but also with the definitions of the scale steps. He should be able to keep in mind the universe of ratings to be made; this should be helpful in organizing the available diagnostic data during their interpretation.

*Second,* test data, interview records, or whatever material is to be used, should be interpreted and the interpretations organized in such a fashion that it is possible to relate them to the variables in the scheme.

*Third,* the ratings expressing the position of the individual assessed on each of the scales are noted down. In general, it is helpful to proceed in the order in which the scales appear in the scheme because of their increasing order of complexity. Occasionally, however, a specific aspect of a person, encompassed in a scale appearing later in the scheme, is so pronounced or obvious that one may wish to make a relevant rating first of all. A word of caution should be added: while, because of the roughly hierarchical order of the scales, some ratings on later ones may partly be based on ratings on earlier scales, it would be contrary to the logic of the scheme to let ratings on the less complex variables (such as Ideational Styles) be influenced by ratings on the more complex dimensions (such as Character Elaborations).

An important issue in using the rating scales concerns reference populations. There are no "norms" available for them, either in terms of age, or sex, or of socio-economic or cultural status. To a degree it seems that the scale and step-definitions are sufficiently specific to provide a standard against which to make a rating. In some measure, however, it may also be necessary for an investigator to draw on his knowledge of a particular age or sex group which he may be studying. This is perhaps particularly important for making ratings on Psychosocial Modalities, Femininity vs. Masculinity, and a few others. Related is the issue of "normality" or, better expressed, of optimal positions on the scales. The steps for each scale were defined in such a way that they would span as much as possible the entire expectable range of the variable represented in the scale. No particular attempt was made to let any step stand for a "normal" position but in most cases a step near the middle such as 3, 3.5, and, relatively often even 4 may be adaptively "optimal." Which step represents an optimum may vary from scale to scale. "Normality," at any rate, should not be assumed to be some sort of arithmetical sum or average of ratings; but should be judged, if at all, only in terms of a configurational appreciation of the total of a particular person's functioning.

It happens fairly often that more than one rating on a given scale is appropriate to a representation of the data available of a subject. In such cases split-ratings or sub-ratings may be given. If, for instance, both step 2 and step 4 are applicable, the rating would be written as 2–4. Should the rating be predominantly 1.5 but there are also noteworthy trends represented by step 4, it would be recorded as $1.5_4$. Half-point ratings such as 2.5 are permissible and are frequently used to indicate an intermediate position on the scale steps.

The next chapter presents an index of the dimensions contained in our assessment scheme which is followed by the actual scales with their definitions. In the later chapters two illustrative case studies are presented which are hoped to exemplify the rating procedures; one of them uses test data, the other an interview protocol.

# RATING SCALES FOR CHARACTEROLOGICAL ASSESSMENT

## INDEX OF CATEGORIES

**A. Ideational Styles**
1. *Cognitive reactivity*
2. *Originality*
3. *Abstractness*
4. *Lability*
5. *Attentiveness*

**B. Prominent Affects**
1. *Depression*
2. *Guilt*
3. *Affection and love*
4. *Shame*
5. *Frustration and thwartedness, dissatisfaction*
6. *Elation*
7. *Anxiety*
8. *Hostility*

**C. Prominent Defenses**
1. *Repression*
2. *Denial*
3. *Projection*
4. *Reaction formation*

5. *Isolation*
6. *Intellectualization*
7. *Rationalization*
8. *Undoing*
9. *Introjection and identification*
      a. With aggressor
      b. Altruistic
10. *Over-all defensive success*

**D. Superego**
1. *Severity*
2. *Integration*

**E. Adaptive Strengths**
1. *Adequacy of reality testing*
2. *Degree of synthesis within the ego*
3. *Stress tolerance*
4. *Amount of committable energy available for adaptive tasks*
5. *Strength and variety of experienced affects*
      a. Strength
      b. Variety and complexity
6. *Profundity and variety of thought contents*
      a. Profundity
      b. Variety
7. *Regression in the service of the ego*
      a. Over-all rating
      b. Creative output
      c. Wit, humor, and playfulness
8. *Social adaptiveness*
      a. Ability to change oneself
      b. Ability to change or influence others
      c. Flexibility of social exploration and affiliation
      d. State of social adaptation (pleasurable related-ness)
9. *Drive regulation, utilization, and implementation*

**F. Sense of Self**
1. *Control vs. being influenced*
2. *Involvement (active or passive) vs. detachment*
3. *Expansion of relations with the not-self vs. constriction*

4. *Homogeneity of the self vs. conflict*
5. *Body image*
6. *Acceptance of the self vs. rejection*

**G. Psychosocial Modalities**
A. *Subject's standing on each modality*
   1. Trust vs. basic mistrust
   2. Autonomy vs. shame and doubt
   3. Initiative vs. guilt
   4. Industry vs. inferiority
   5. Identity vs. identity diffusion
   6. Intimacy vs. isolation
   7. Generativity vs. stagnation
B. *Degree of emphasis of each modality*
   1. Trust vs. basic mistrust
   2. Autonomy vs. shame and doubt
   3. Initiative vs. guilt
   4. Industry vs. inferiority
   5. Identity vs. identity diffusion
   6. Intimacy vs. isolation
   7. Generativity vs. stagnation

**H. Character Elaborations**
1. *Narcissistic*
2. *Hysterical*
3. *Obsessive*
4. *Feminine-masculine*
5. *Dependent*
6. *Sado-masochistic*
7. *Passive-aggressive*
8. *Hypomanic*
9. *Schizoid*
10. *Projective*
11. *Psychopathic*
12. *Diffusion*
13. *As-if*
14. *Counterphobic*
15. *Depressive*
16. *Genital* (psychosocial and psychosexual maturity)

For suggestions concerning the rating procedure see Chapter 3, particularly pp. 40 and 41.

## THE SCALES

### A. Ideational Styles

1. *Cognitive reactivity* (facility of perception, association, and expression)

    1. Inhibited, blocked, meager
    2. Mildly constricted, occasional spontaneity
    3. Spontaneous, fluent
    4. Very rapid, tendency toward overresponsiveness
    5. Overproductive, flighty
    X. Cannot say
    Comments:

2. *Originality* (refers to unusual ideas or responses rather than to clever elaboration of commonplace material)

    1. Overconventional conformity, drab, naïve, cliché
    2. Some originality and creativity
    3. Original, creative, colorful
    4. Powerfully creative; individual twist
    5. Idiosyncratic, bizarre, florid
    X. Cannot say
    Comments:

3. *Abstractness*

    1. Concretistic, circumstantial, overmeticulous
    2. Detail-oriented, precise, meticulous
    3. Appropriately abstract with sufficient detail
    4. Highly general abstractions with some neglect of detail
    5. Overgeneralized or loose abstractions
    X. Cannot say
    Comments:

4. *Lability*

    1. Labile, dominated by affect, dramatizing, impulsive
    2. Moved by affect, influenced by emotions

    3. Expressive but adequately controlled and orderly
    4. Sober, constricted, dry, unemotional
    5. Rigid, dogmatic, overrationalistic, overly scrupulous
    X. Cannot say
    Comments:

5. *Attentiveness*

    1. Hyperalert to stimuli and conditions in life circumstances to the detriment of grasping the essentials of the situation
    2. Acute awareness of subtleties and minor aspects of a situation
    3. Objectiveness, factual, flexible attentiveness to the essentials of life circumstances
    4. Some unawareness and neglect of important aspects of a situation
    5. Active avoidance of or insensitivity to stimuli and conditions in life circumstances
    X. Cannot say
    Comments:

## B. Prominent Affects

Each rating should be a combination of the subject's experienced and expressed affect. Cite if possible degree of provocation, source of provocation, object, possible qualifications for rating, idiosyncratic expression of particular affects, specific bodily concomitants of particular affects (blushing, sweating, peculiar movements of body, etc.).

1. *Depression*

    1. Little or none
    2. Slight, momentary, less than appropriate depression
    3. Moderate degree of depression
    4. Marked degree of depression, quite unhappy, low mood frequently
    5. Severely depressed. (Experienced: utter worthlessness, helplessness, utter misery. Expressed: crying spells, unable to work)

X. Cannot say
Comments:

## 2. *Guilt*

1. Little or none
2. Mild
3. Moderate guilt reactions
4. Frequent and strong guilt
5. Very intense guilt
X. Cannot say
Comments:

## 3. *Affection and love*

1. No giving or accepting of one's own loving feelings
2. Slight involvement
3. Moderate degree of giving or accepting of one's own loving feelings
4. Strong, passionate
5. Intense absorption in the experience and/or expression of love
X. Cannot say
Comments:

## 4. *Shame* (experience of sense of helpless exposure)

1. No shame or self-consciousness regardless of circumstance
2. Slight, momentary shame
3. Definite but appropriate feelings and/or expression of shame
4. Frequent and strong feelings or expression of shame
5. Extremely ashamed, feelings of humiliation or of helpless exposure
X. Cannot say
Comments:

## 5. *Frustration and thwartedness, dissatisfaction*

1. Satisfaction and gratification in all activities and life in general
2. Mild feelings of frustration and thwartedness

3. Moderate, or occasional but intense, feelings of frustration and thwartedness
4. Frequent feelings of frustration and thwartedness
5. Chronically frustrated and thwarted
X. Cannot say
Comments:

6. *Elation*

1. Bland, consistently sober, serious
2. Mild or momentary elation
3. Elated at appropriate times, generally good spirits, cheerful
4. Exaggerated degree of happiness, "high" a considerable portion of time, often inappropriately elated (in face of reversals, unhappy events)
5. Hypomanic, "nothing bothers him," completely dominated by inappropriate elation
X. Cannot say
Comments:

7. *Anxiety*

1. Bland, totally unconcerned and unthreatened by any event
2. Mild concern, usually with reference to certain objects
3. Fairly frequently apprehensive and nervous, sometimes not related to specific situation
4. A worrier, many situations anxiety-producing, or specific phobic reactions, difficulty in concentrating at work
5. Overwrought by anxiety, adequate functioning of any kind is difficult, definite phobias
X. Cannot say
Comments:

8. *Hostility*

1. Never hostile or angry, regardless of circumstances
2. Infrequent hostile feelings or expressions
3. Does get mad at times
4. Easily stimulated into angry feelings or feelings of fury
5. Intense and persistent hostility with little or no provocation

X. Cannot say
Comments:

## C. Prominent Defenses

### 1. *Repression*

1. Relatively light (can appear as unusual freedom of inner awareness)
2. Ordinary, undistinguished (no marked defensive impoverishment of current internal experience and/or memory; fantasy, self-confrontation, intellectual curiosity, etc., are tolerable)
3. Moderate
4. Strong
5. Very strong
X. Cannot say

Comments: Note particular drives, memories, fantasies, affects especially to be repressed or breaking through repressions. Are breakthroughs occasional or chronic?

### 2. *Denial*

1. Minimal, extraordinarily attentive to internal and external conditions
2. Ordinary, undistinguished
3. Moderate
4. Strong
5. Extreme, intensive and extensive (extreme hypomanic or Pollyanna-type denials and reversals of painful realities)
X. Cannot say

Comments: Is emphasis more hypomanic (with elevated mood, pressure of speech, flightiness, etc.) or Pollyanna-ish (with tranquil, peaceful, contented, conflictless emphasis)? What is the particular content to be denied?

### 3. *Projection*

1. Minimal
2. Ordinary, undistinguished (useful in empathy and alertness and disruptive only occasionally and moderately under stress)

3. Moderate, significant tendency towards complaintiveness

4. Strong (strong social anxiety and defensiveness, mistrustfulness, hyperalertness; vulnerable to marked distortions under stress)

5. Extreme, intensive and extensive (subject shows paranoid-fixed ideas or frequent marked distortions of a suspicious or grandiose nature)

X. Cannot say

Comments: Is emphasis on grandiosity or suspiciousness primarily, or mixed? Note particular content to be projected in two respects:

a. id content or superego content primarily, or mixed?

b. specific drive content emphasized such as hostility, homosexuality, dependency, narcissism, etc.

4. *Reaction formation*

1. Minimal (frequently evidences slovenly, smutty, cruel patterns)

2. Ordinary, undistinguished (sufficient for adequate but not conspicuous orderliness, cleanliness, tenderness, etc.)

3. Moderate

4. Strong

5. Extreme, intensive and extensive (extremely orderly, clean, over-considerate, prurient)

X. Cannot say

Comments: Underline words best describing form of appearance of defense: orderly, perfectionistic, conscientious, tender and deferent, sincere and self-searching, ascetic, pseudomasculine, pseudofeminine, self-sufficient. Specify content to be warded off.

5. *Isolation* (defense against affect appropriate to concrete, important personal and interpersonal events)

1. Minimal

2. Ordinary, undistinguished (sufficient for adequate application and efficiency in a variety of tasks calling for concentration and objectivity)

    3. Moderate

    4. Strong

    5. Extreme, intensive and extensive (minimal awareness of affect and/or relation of affects to precipitating situations; aversion towards affects; striving for complete detachment, objectivity, calm)

    X. Cannot say

    Comments:

**6. *Intellectualization*** (referring to abstract, esoteric, and logical interpretations of internal and external conditions)

    1. Minimal

    2. Ordinary, undistinguished

    3. Moderate

    4. Strong

    5. Extreme (all internal and external events are interpreted philosophically and logically to the exclusion of emotional considerations)

    X. Cannot say

    Comments:

**7. *Rationalization*** (referring to common sense, utilitarian justifications of internal and external conditions)

    1. Minimal

    2. Ordinary, undistinguished

    3. Moderate

    4. Strong

    5. Extreme

    X. Cannot say

    Comments:

**8. *Undoing***

    1. Not present or observable

    2. Present (there are atonements with magical, superstitious elements; compulsive rituals)

    Comments:

**9. *Introjection and identification***

    a. With aggressor

1. Minimal; sadomasochistic orientation, emphasis on victimization
2. Ordinary, undistinguished (some tendency under marked stress)
3. Moderate
4. Strong
5. Extreme (rigid, unyielding insistence on active, aggressive role)
X. Cannot say

Comments: Specify content of identification(s) if prominent, e.g., counterphobic, tyrannical, sadistic, etc.

b. Altruistic

1. Minimal (avoids altruistic involvement)
2. Ordinary (does not actively seek out altruistic relationships and insist on them, but some tendency evident in close relationships)
3. Moderate
4. Strong
5. Extreme (can only relate to others and derive pleasure through their gratifications and attainments; pathological selflessness)
X. Cannot say

Comments: Specify content of altruism, e.g., love, success, etc.

10. *Over-all defensive success*

1. Very weak
2. Spotty
3. Moderately successful
4. Adequate and flexible
5. Overly rigid
X. Cannot say

Comments:

## D. Superego

1. *Severity* (estimate according to:

   a. Vulnerability
   b. Severity of guilt, expressed and inferred

    c. Rigidity and severity of defenses

Indications of latent guilt should include self-punitive behaviors and attitudes [injury, derogation, failure] and their opposites [sanctimoniousness, exaggerated self-esteem] and mood disturbances [low and high])

1. Minimal indications (absense of appropriate sense of responsibility; suggestion of ingrained psychopathy)
2. Relatively weak
3. Moderate (appropriate guilt and some neurotic guilt but no great instability of self-esteem, no great intolerance for the affect, and efforts made to take relatively appropriate actions to correct the situation)
4. Strong
5. Severe (very vulnerable to severe guilt and/or extreme defensive ego constriction to avoid guilt and/or extreme denials)
X. Cannot say
Comments:

2. *Integration* (estimate according to unity or absence of contradiction between standards and behavior and also among standards)

1. Behavior generally consistent with standards; standards relatively consistent
2. Definite inconsistencies and/or contradictions
3. Extreme inconsistencies and/or contradictions (e.g., "corrupt superego")
X. Cannot say
Comments: Indicate area of discrepancy if possible.

# E. Adaptive Strengths

1. *Adequacy of reality testing* (internal and external)

1. Inadequate, pathological distortion
2. Fairly frequent, marked lapses, some self-correction occurs, continuous moderate distortion
3. Occasional lapses, or mild disregard of certain reality aspects

4. Definitely adequate, appropriately comprehensive perception of reality
5. Overly alert reality emphasis, pedantic, inflexible
X. Cannot say
Comments:

2. *Degree of synthesis within the ego* (absence of unreconciled contradictions or divergencies within experience, self-organization and behavior)

1. Minimal, there is general fragmentation, contradiction and diffusion
2. Some degree of synthesis in part areas; major areas, however, remain unintegrated
3. Fair degree of synthesis of major areas and trends but some aspects remain definitely unintegrated
4. On the whole there is quite consistent over-all synthesis, only minor unintegrated aspects remain, making for variety
5. Exaggerated and rigid degree of synthesis, leading to lack of complexity or variety of psychic structure; pseudointegration
X. Cannot say
Comments:

3. *Stress tolerance*

1. Weak or none at all; even minor stress leads to almost complete disorganization and breakdown of functioning
2. Fair: Small stresses can be handled but the ordinary major life difficulties are met with considerable disturbance, disruption, and inefficiency of functioning
3. Adequate: Most stresses can be handled fairly well but major ones produce some disturbance and temporary deterioration of functioning
4. Considerable: Most expectable stresses can be dealt with successfully without disruption of functioning
5. Very high: No evidence that any predictable stress will lead to any disturbance; pathological lack of reactivity
X. Cannot say
Comments:

4. *Amount of committable energy available for adaptive tasks* (for example, in terms of work effort, enthusiasm, efficiency of intellectual functioning)

1. None at all; no output of any kind; completely absorbed in simple life processes or in autistic preoccupations
2. Little: Capable to direct his attention to small and simple problems of short duration and ease of solution; not much persistence
3. Fair: Problems of moderate size are accepted and carried through with some degree of personal involvement; needs "rest" and "recovery" periods
4. Considerable: Capable of sustained effort and involvement, persistent; can handle several problems at a time and carry them through
5. Maximal: Involvements have a "driven" quality; enormous energy either scattered over too wide an area or invested in a restricted narrow area; inefficiency in terms of over-all adaptation results in both cases

X. Cannot say
Comments:

5. *Strength and variety of experienced affects*

a. Strength

1. Minimal: Lack or near lack of affective responsiveness, cold, blank, frozen, machine-like, apathetic
2. Low: Affective experience is weak and rare but it does occur
3. Moderate: Definite presence of an affective "tone," relatively contained affective responsiveness
4. Considerable: Responsive, emotional, easily moved, stimulated, influenced by marked affects over periods of time
5. Maximal: Hypersensitive, explosive, carried away almost constantly; being completely dominated by an unchanging, severe affect

X. Cannot say
Comments:

b. Variety and complexity

1. None: No discernible variety in affective states
2. Little: Occasional changes in quality of affective experience but within very restricted general range
3. Moderate: Able to experience an ordinary variety and some complexity of the usual household affects
4. Considerable: Differential, affective responses to a quite wide variety of situations or ideas
5. Extreme: Very many, hardly classifiable, highly personal, complicated shadings of affective experience
X. Cannot say
Comments:

6. *Profundity and variety of thought contents*

a. Profundity

1. Extremely shallow, concrete, things are considered entirely by their face value; automatic, stereotyped approach to any problem
2. Tends to be shallow; the meaning of any situation or idea is examined only occasionally or under pressure; most things taken for granted
3. Moderate: Some things taken for granted but in some areas analysis occurs
4. Considerable: Habitual inclination not to take things or ideas by their surface value; analyzes; is concerned with implications, meanings, and relevance
5. Extreme preoccupation with all possible implications, meanings, and relations; highly abstract, philosophical; others find it difficult or impossible to follow him
X. Cannot say
Comments:

b. Variety

1. Minimal: Obsessed with one thing, fixed idea, perseverative
2. Some: Varying thought contents within a narrow area
3. Moderate: Fairly wide variation of thought contents over a number of areas

4. Considerable: Wide variety of thought contents, richness, fluidity
5. Maximal: Distractible, rapid transitions, scattered, concerned with widely distant matters, farfetchedness
X. Cannot say
Comments:

7. *Regression in the service of the ego*

a. Over-all rating

1. Minimal: Rigid adherence to standards of realism, efficiency, practicality, logicality, seriousness
2. Occasional, unwilling, hesitant, surprised concern with internal, irrational experience, not much utilization of such experience
3. Some access to and use of personal, irrational material (feelings, images) which is accepted as existent and part of the self
4. Considerable access to personal, irrational material, utilization of it for flexible, imaginative solutions to adaptive problems, creative output
5. Maximal: Frequent and intense immersion in personal, irrational material, encroachment of ego-alien material, difficulty in recovering realistic orientation, only spotty utilization of the material for adaptive solutions
X. Cannot say
Comments:

b. Creative output (intellectually, artistically, in the sense of producing something new)

1. Minimal: No originality; output in any area is stereotyped, conforming to established routine, machine-like
2. Some: Occasional instances of minor creativeness occur but they are disconnected and usually not carried through to a finished product
3. Moderate: Instances of creativeness leading to productions of modest size occur sufficiently often to play a role in the person's life
4. Considerable creative output leading to valuable productions; frequent and continuous stream of creation;

the person's existence is based on it to an important degree

5. Maximal: Almost incessant, "driven" output beyond the person's capacity to regulate and guide it; productions may or may not be acceptable by usual standards of value

X. Cannot say

Comments:

c. Wit, humor, and playfulness

1. Minimal: Dry, no sense of humor, "can't relax" or play at all
2. Some: Occasional, unexpected instances of humor or play which seem out of keeping with the person's general behavior
3. Moderate: Some sense of humor, witticisms, etc., on certain occasions or under facilitating circumstances, able to play
4. Known as a witty and humorous person, well able to relax and play with enjoyment
5. Continuously joking, no seriousness, plays all the time, not capable of organizing his energies for any purpose beyond immediate pleasure

X. Cannot say

Comments:

8. *Social adaptiveness*

a. Ability to change oneself (autoplastic)

1. Minimal: Extreme rigidity, uncompromising, refusal or inability to change
2. Little: Only in very limited areas or under great pressure some change occurs which may not be maintained beyond duration of pressure
3. Moderate: Change may occur in some areas if definite pressure or need for it is present
4. Considerable: Changes of the self occur fairly easily and fluidly, leading to good fitting into the total social situation; important characteristics and valued orientations, however, are maintained

     5. Extreme: Chameleon-like adaptability, no stability or constancy in the personality; extremely fluid changes even with minor and unessential situational pressure

    X. Cannot say

    Comments:

b. Ability to change or influence others (alloplastic, by means of persuasion, pressure, prestige)

    1. Minimal: No dominance, leadership, does not influence others at all

    2. Some: Occasionally in minor issues manages to influence others

    3. Moderate: Influences others in issues of not very great importance or breadth, or at times is influential in important matters

    4. Considerable: Is on the whole a leading figure or a persuasive one; frequently succeeds in influencing others even in major issues

    5. Extreme: Has others completely in his hand, can make them do almost anything he wants, strikingly influential, his influence completely accepted by others, has almost magic powers

    X. Cannot say

    Comments:

c. Flexibility of social exploration and affiliation

    1. Minimal: Social affiliation is with a relatively limited and quite unchanged group; no new contacts are attempted

    2. Little: Group affiliations remain mostly unchanged, only very occasionally new contacts are attempted or made

    3. Moderate: A limited number of new contacts are attempted or made, certain stable affiliations remain dominant

    4. Considerable: While there are some stable affiliations, new contacts are frequently attempted and often successful

5. Extreme: Butterfly behavior, tumbles from one group to the next, constantly makes new contacts and affiliations of short duration; no stability

X. Cannot say

Comments:

d. State of social adaptation (pleasurable relatedness)

1. Minimal: General unpleasure and/or withdrawal
2. Some pleasure in being with other people but infrequent or weak
3. Frequent pleasurable contacts with people; in general favorably oriented towards them
4. Relations to others are main and substantial source of pleasure, other interests are subordinated to this
5. Socially hyperactive with only superficial involvement and flight from the self

X. Cannot say

Comments:

9. *Drive regulation, utilization, and implementation* (specify qualitatively which drives)

1. Minimal: Almost completely a victim of any impulse, unable to delay or control gratification
2. Little: Occasionally able to postpone gratification or to control and channel drives but impulsive and labile most of the time
3. Moderate: More often than not able to impose delays and conditions of gratification upon his impulses, gratifications fit social conditions much of the time
4. Considerable: Well able to postpone gratifications and to fit them into social contexts; enjoys gratifications, can anticipate them with pleasure and utilize them for favorable over-all adaptation
5. Maximal: Complete control over impulses, can "switch them on and off," uses them for rationally expressed purposes; loss of spontaneity and genuineness

X. Cannot say

Comments:

## F. Sense of Self

The following variables refer to the manner in which a person senses himself to be in his total relationship to the not-self. The not-self includes certain internal phenomena and forces as well as external ones of a social, physical, or abstract nature. The first three variables focus on the over-all qualities of interaction with the not-self; the remaining three, on the way the subject sees the self as one pole in the relation to the not-self. The ratings are to be made on the basis of any evidence relating to a subject's predominantly and relatively more consciously held sense of self. If certain data should suggest the inference of a latent sense of self that is very different from that experienced or expressed by the subject, this should be stated under "Comments."

1. *Control vs. being influenced*

    1. All relationships with the not-self are sensed to be completely under one's active control, influence, and direction; this may border on to or include a sense of omnipotence or grandiosity
    2. Relationships with the not-self are primarily sensed to be under one's control and determination but occasional modification of the self is sensed to occur under the influence of the not-self
    3. The relationship with the not-self is sensed to be partly under the control and determination of the self but the self is also sensed as being influenced to a significant degree by the not-self
    4. The self is sensed as mostly under the influence of the not-self but in limited areas or degrees it still exerts some control and direction
    5. The self is sensed to be completely under the influence or at the mercy of the not-self; there may be an experience of being overwhelmed, swept away, completely subjugated, etc.
    X. Cannot say
    Comments:

2. *Involvement (active or passive) vs. detachment*

    1. Dominating sense of involvement with almost every-

thing; the self relates intensely to every aspect or content of the not-self; the border between self and not-self is blurred in wide areas; "oceanic feeling"

2. Strong involvement with a broad variety of areas of the not-self; subject is a "self-less" person but is capable of or maintains some detachment in minor areas

3. Definite involvement with some areas or aspects of the not-self but there is also detachment from a significant part of the not-self

4. Detachment predominates; it includes a definite sense of distinction between the self and the not-self; some areas of involvement with the not-self remain

5. Complete detachment; there is withdrawal, self-absorption, a sense of an unbridgeable gap, and a lack of responsiveness with regard to the not-self

X. Cannot say

Comments:

3. *Expansion of relations with the not-self vs. constriction*

1. An intense and frantic sense of continuing and rapid indiscriminate expansion, of wholesale exploration and assimilation of new phenomena, issues, relations, etc.

2. Marked sense of strong but definitely directed and discriminating expansion of relationships

3. Sense of expansion is present with regard to some areas of the not-self but on the whole the number and intensity of relationships remain the same

4. The breadth and number of relationships with certain areas of the not-self are sensed as remaining constant, but other relationships are sensed as being or having been discontinued

5. Marked sense of continuing and progressive abandonment of relationships with the not-self

X. Cannot say

Comments:

4. *Homogeneity of the self vs. conflict*

1. The self is sensed as being completely harmonious, peaceful, and lacking in conflict within itself

2. Sense of harmoniousness and homogeneity of the self predominates but inner areas of conflict are also experienced

3. Some harmoniousness and the presence of certain conflict-free areas in the self are sensed as well as some areas of definite and significant conflict

4. A sense of internal conflict prevails but there remain some areas of harmony and stability

5. There is an overwhelming sense of conflict and struggle, nothing in the self seems stable, secure, or peaceful

X. Cannot say

Comments:

5. *Body image*

1. The body is highly overvalued; there may be a conviction of its perfection and beauty; its enhancement and care are a major purpose in life

2. The body is considered important as a well-functioning and dependable tool or asset; there is satisfaction with the body

3. The body is considered all right and on the whole functioning appropriately; there is no great preoccupation with it

4. The body is disregarded or neglected; or it may be sensed as imperfect in some respects, is disliked, devalued, and not considered an asset

5. The body is felt to be strange, possessed by uncontrollable and/or malicious forces; it may be felt to be malfunctioning or disintegrating or to be diseased; bizarre body preoccupations may appear

X. Cannot say

Comments:

6. *Acceptance of the self vs. rejection*

1. Complete, unqualified satisfaction with the self; a sense that one can do no wrong; is perfect, and in no need of any change

2. General satisfaction with the self but some sense of personal weaknesses and possibilities for improvement

3. Satisfaction and dissatisfaction with the self may alternate or are both present with regard to different characteristics or attributes of the self
4. Dissatisfaction predominates; a sense of not being lovable, worthwhile, or much good; self-reproaches and self-depreciation; wish to be different may be present
5. Complete dissatisfaction with the self; no hope of any chance of improvement, sense of being beyond salvation and of being a burden to the world; strong trends towards self-destruction

X. Cannot say

Comments:

## G. Psychosocial Modalities

The following seven variables concern complex phenomena and are not intended to be independent from one another. Since they represent issues arising at subsequent stages of development it follows that the successful solution of later developmental crises is dependent to a considerable degree on a successful solution of the earlier ones. Thus, evidence for these ratings should be drawn from several levels.

### A. *Subject's standing on each modality*

### 1. *Trust vs. basic mistrust*

*Trust* may be defined as a deeply ingrained conviction that one's needs, material and emotional, will be satisfied; that the world and the people in it are basically good, abundant in their supplies, and well-meaning. But it also implies a personal feeling of "being all right" oneself, and of being considered all right by significant others; a feeling that one can cope with the world and with oneself, and that one is at home in one's body. Finally, it implies a confident feeling that requirements and even frustrations coming from the outside generally make sense.

*Basic mistrust* may be defined as a sense of always living precariously, that good things never last, that one does not know if one's needs will be satisfied tomorrow and rather doubts that they will be. That the world contains many hidden dangers, that people are out to exploit or even "get" you; that oneself is bad and empty, can't cope, and is doomed to suffer failure and injury; that the world is an unsafe, unpredictable, threatening and cold place.

The trust *vs.* mistrust issue is also considered to be an acute one if there appears in the record a marked emphasis on orality as expressed in concerns over such matters as food, nourishment, dependence, nourishing persons, etc. These concerns may appear in a benevolent form, indicating a more passive and naïve form of trust or a denial or frustration of dependency. If these oral concerns appear in a more aggressive and destructive context (demandingness, greediness, teeth, devouring, gnawing, etc.), mistrust would seem implied.

A more successful solution of this developmental issue would be indicated by some not extreme and not too primitively expressed or too conflicted manifestations of oral concerns. Ratings would then tend towards 2 or 3.

*Scale:*

1. The subject is entirely trusting in a naïve, childish, and unrealistic, if benevolent way; is a kind of guileless fool

2. Trust predominates markedly, but there are some realistic limitations, some cautiousness; occasional, moderate, relatively brief crises in significant relationships

3. Trust and mistrust keep an approximate balance in their frequency and intensity; there may be vacillation between instances of predominating trust or mistrust

4. Mistrust predominates markedly, but some concessions are made at times. The world and people are given an occasional chance

5. Pathological mistrust entirely dominates the picture; it may assume delusional proportions

X. Cannot say

Comments:

## 2. *Autonomy vs. shame and doubt*

*Autonomy* can be defined as a sense that one is capable of being and may be the originator of one's own actions; that one has a will of one's own and can exercise it; that one "stands on his own feet"; that one is in control of oneself and exercises this control comfortably; it includes a sense of pride and independence, and of being able to hold one's ground in the face of others.

*Shame and doubt* refers to a sense of being easily exposed as powerless, incapable, weak, and bad. It includes a wish to hide from others, to cover up one's despicability and worthlessness. One's own plans and actions are surrounded by doubts concerning their justification, value and efficacy. Self-consciousness and a lack of self-confidence are present; inability to make up one's mind.

If this issue is prominent, there may be a marked emphasis on anality as expressed in concerns with the following, or their opposites: Orderliness, cleanliness, regulation and scheduling of things, balance, tenderness, utility, parsimony and efficiency, authority and compliance. Also emphasis on hiding, covering-up, being seen, exposed. Representation of and concern with the excretory organs and their products, with retention and elimination. Refined, deliberate, and controlled forms of sadism, or masochism. Stubbornness, dutifulness.

*Scale:*

1. An exaggerated sense of autonomy, self-importance, and omnipotence is present. Realistic limitations are disregarded, social maladaptation may result

2. A strong sense of autonomy is present, but some of its limitations are recognized and occasional self-doubting occurs. An "independent" personality

3. The proportion of autonomy and doubt or shame is about even. One or the other predominates on different occasions, but the crises are not extreme enough to cause maladaptation

4. Doubt and shame predominate; a self-conscious, indecisive person tending to apologize for his existence,

but sufficient autonomy is present to deal marginally and very effortfully with normal life situations. Possible rebelliousness against own insignificant status and against authority

5. Extreme degree of shame and doubtfulness. Continuous wish to sink into the ground and disappear, no sense of capability for any self-originated action. Sense of being worth nothing and doing everything badly. Possibly marked rebelliousness against authority

X. Cannot say

Comments:

## 3. *Initiative vs. guilt*

*Initiative* refers to: evidence of ambition, energetic driving in pursuit of accomplishment, a tendency to solve problems by attack, pleasure in attack and conquest, striving towards goals lying in the future, but also to active, curious exploration and active, expansive movement; rivalrous, and jealous competition.

*Guilt* is here understood specifically as guilt over enjoyment derived from acts of "making," and over the aggressive components of active competition. Excessive guilt would be manifested by self-restriction, overconscientiousness in planning enterprises, and paralysis of action.

This issue would also be reflected in emphasis on representations of sexual organs, their adequacy and intactness, as well as of the body in general, especially in terms of showing and showing off.

With *men* the accent would lie on intrusion of a physical, intellectual, and social sort, on "making" by invading, monopolizing, and manipulating of people and things.

In *women* the emphasis would lie on "making" by inception, maternal inclusion, or creation. Also on seductive, bitchy, bodily-narcissistic demandingness for attention to her as a physical being.

Negatively, in both sexes may be found: fear of damage, confinement, weakness, losing out to rivals, or a sense that all these should occur or have already occurred. In women also: being found unattractive, unlovable, repulsive.

*Scale:*

1. Exaggerated initiative, constantly striving for new goals, full of plans, hard-driving, unscrupulously forging ahead, "big operator."
2. Initiative predominates, is in general moderated, guided, or influenced by considerations of conscience, but the latter are not inhibiting in an unrealistic way
3. Initiative and guilt are in approximate balance. At times initiative has the upper hand and new goals are striven for; at times pursuits are inhibited by somewhat unrealistic considerations of conscience, or are laden with guilt.
4. Guilt predominates, inhibiting the choice and active pursuit of new goals considerably. There is marked restriction and paralysis of initiative.
5. Excessive guilt. Almost completely blocked in all forms of enterprise to the degree of actual, symbolic, or symptomatic self-injury

X. Cannot say

Comments:

### 4. *Industry vs. inferiority*

*Industry* refers to an active orientation towards producing things and thus to win recognition. There is eager absorption in the productive situation and determined striving towards the completion of things; "stick-to-it-iveness." There are sincere attempts to be useful and to do useful things. Skills are acquired, practiced, and valued. There is marked interest in learning how things are done in the surrounding culture from the points of view of know-how and/or rules.

*Inferiority* refers to a despairing of one's tools and skills, leading to a sense of being unable to be like others, of being doomed to mediocrity or of being crippled, mutilated, and isolated.

*Scale:*

1. Excessive industry; use of production and persevering work as exclusive means towards achievement of a

place in society at the cost of direct human contact and leading to impoverishment in other areas of life. Feels that everything can be accomplished with sufficient persistence and energy

2. Industry predominates. Engages persistently in energetic production but admits that he cannot do everything and has certain limitations

3. Industry and inferiority in about equal proportions. There are skills and productive drive in some areas, while lack of ability and interest for other areas are perceived by the subject; or the drive may be coupled with a sense of inferiority

4. Inferiority predominates. A general sense of inability and lack of skill is present, but there are exceptions. In certain relatively narrow areas or at certain times production does occur with some degree of proficiency

5. A sense of overwhelming inferiority in all areas predominates. The subject feels generally incapable, poorly equipped, and thus isolated.

X. Cannot say

Comments:


## 5. Identity vs. identity diffusion

*Identity* refers to a sense of inner sameness and continuity in time, and of inner homogeneity at any given point in time. Specifically it implies a sense of being at home in one's body, of "knowing where one is going," and of an assuredness of recognition by others. All this is based on good integration between inner drives and wishes, and social conditions, specifically in terms of work, sex, relationships to peers, and the community.

*Identity diffusion* implies a sense of discrepancy between one's appearance and being, doubts concerning one's sexual identity, an inability to choose a career because of conflicting interests and doubts, an inability to relate to others as an equal partner or to compete with them, a feeling of emptiness, lack of a coherent philosophy of life and of a goal for one's existence. No commitments are made and a state of paralysis with regard to the making of choices exists.

*Scale:*

1. Rigidly developed identity with a maximum of internal homogeneity; nearly all psychological structures and functions are forcibly integrated with and attuned to limited aspects of the present environment. Implied is an arrest of development at this stage which leaves little possibility for future change; there are no dormant potentials left
2. Well developed identity and good social integration. However, some unintegrated capacities, wishes, etc., remain
3. Moderately developed identity. Some of the time or in some major areas there is fairly good integration between personal factors and the social surroundings; at other times or in some areas it is lacking. Occasional crises.
4. Identity diffusion predominates. Only occasional or partial integration of personal factors with surrounding society; internal conflict and indecision or presence of a moderately negative (autistic, oppositional) identity.
5. General identity diffusion. No integrated picture of the self, its qualities, purposes, and goals at all. Much internal contradiction and conflict, and lacking or very poor integration of personal wishes, capabilities, etc., with the surrounding society; or presence of markedly negative identity

X. Cannot say
   Comments:

## 6. *Intimacy vs. isolation*

*Intimacy* refers to a capacity for full mutuality with a loved partner. This includes ability to achieve full orgasms, but also to share mutual trust and to regulate together the "cycles of work, procreation, and recreation." All this is based on an ability to face "ego loss" with others as well as within oneself (in the form of orgasm, abandon, giving oneself up to inspiration, intuition, etc.)

*Isolation* refers to a sense of having to remain alone and of being self-absorbed, on the basis of the fear of ego loss. Social relations remain formal or abortive, sexual relations lack emotional mutuality.

*Scale:*

1. Full capacity for intimacy as shown by the fact that the subject has achieved it
2. Capacity for intimacy appears to be definitely present; no lasting intimate relationship is as yet achieved, but successful experimentation with such relationships is being undertaken
3. Intimacy and isolation are present in about equal degrees; there is vacillation between these two poles
4. Isolation is predominant. Occasional attempts at intimacy remain abortive or are of short duration
5. The subject is fully isolated, self-absorbed, and is not able to or refuses to share anything close to his self with anybody

X. Cannot say
Comments:

### 7. *Generativity vs. stagnation*

*Generativity* refers to a deeply sensed interest and involvement in establishing and guiding the next generation; or, in the absence of actual parental responsibilities, to other concerns of an altruistic and creative quality.

*Stagnation* on the other hand represents an absence of such generative involvement; it may result in an obsessive need for pseudointimacy, in self-indulgence, and be represented in a subjective sense of impoverishment and lack of genuine purpose.

*Scale:*

1. There is full absorption in child care and rearing as the major item of involvement; or a sense of cumulative and creative activity, of building or developing something of major proportions

2. Considerable absorption in generativity but with some doubts and mildly interfering egocentric concerns
3. Generativity is present to some degree but it is absent at times or sensed as a pressing responsibility, and it is conflict-laden
4. Stagnation predominates. The issue of generativity has, in general, been avoided or approached only tentatively. There is no marked involvement in it
5. Over-all stagnation. Complete absence of powerful, reproductive, caring, and creative interest. No purpose, one lives for the moment, and his own short-term gratification

X. Cannot say
Comments:

## B. *Degree of emphasis of each modality*

Here the degree of emphasis is rated with which each psychosocial issue appears in the material regardless of which of its two poles is the more prominent one.

1. Minimal. There is no noteworthy emphasis on the particular modality.
2. Some special emphasis on the particular modality, but not pressing, only occasional manifestations.
3. Fairly strong emphasis; the modality plays definitely a significant role in the person's behavior.
4. Very marked emphasis on the particular modality; issues arising from it dominate a wide range of the person's behavior.
5. Maximal. Concern with issues arising from the particular modality overrides all other concerns, and it appears to dominate, or express itself in almost all of the person's behavior.

Enter a rating on the above scale for each of the following modalities.

1. Trust *vs.* basic mistrust
2. Autonomy *vs.* shame and doubt
3. Initiative *vs.* guilt
4. Industry *vs.* inferiority
5. Identity *vs.* identity diffusion

6. Intimacy *vs.* isolation
7. Generativity *vs.* stagnation

## H. Character Elaborations

Every subject receives a rating for each character type.
All ratings to be made on this scale:

1. Minimal or no evidence of these attributes
2. Some noteworthy instances of these attributes
3. Marked and striking instances of these attributes
4. These attributes form the subject's predominant orientation
5. Subject is a prime example of this configuration of qualities
X. Cannot say
Comments:

### 1. *Narcissistic*

High degree of egocentricity, inability or refusal to "give" emotionally or to empathize with others or to consider seriously anybody's thoughts but one's own; sometimes giving an overt show of interest, social responsiveness, or affective involvement but basically distant, cold, and disinterested.

### 2. *Hysterical*

Tends to be infantile, naïve, emotionally labile (including phobic), impulsive; to be dramatic, histrionic; repressive and possibly "Pollyannic"; tends to sexualize nonsexual relations, to be suggestible. The last may reach such a degree of repudiation of reality and predominance of wishfulness that varying degrees of lying may result.

### 3. *Obsessive*

Pedantic stickler, intellectualizing, perfectionistic, hardheaded, sober, unsentimental, rigid, ruminative, emotionally cold, doubting, unspontaneous, righteous, formalistic, abstractly idealistic.

4. *Feminine vs. masculine* (rate character elaboration opposite to subject's sex)

a. Feminine: Tendency to be yielding, submissive, passive, tender, nurturant, caring, bitchy; feminine interests.

b. Masculine: Tendency to be domineering, intrusive, competitive, exhibitionistic, athletic, tough.

## 5. *Dependent*

Need to have support, care, protection and help from others, inability to get along without these; subtle domination and manipulation of others by forcing them to take responsibility for one, need to have dependable authorities available.

## 6. *Sado-masochistic*

Relationships to others are seen primarily in terms of inflicted or suffered aggression; habitual tendency to inflict mental or physical cruelty; bullying, enjoyment of others' powerlessness; enjoying, seeing value and merit in suffering and sacrifice. Infliction of damage or pain on own self. Either orientation may be predominant, or there may be simultaneous presence or alternation of these two components.

## 7. *Passive-aggressive*

Tendency to deal with the demands of others but also of one's self by means of overt compliance and conformity but at the same time subtle, sneaky, accidental or behind-the-back aggression. Manifestations of passive resistance, procrastination, disguised trickery, or failures.

## 8. *Hypomanic*

Tendency to be overly optimistic, hyperactive, enterprising, benevolent, trustful of one's own potentialities; denying everything bad, painful, unlucky, or difficult as unimportant or nonexistent; driving, pushing others on or around, always full of schemes. Mildly euphoric.

## 9. *Schizoid*

Tends to be withdrawn, distant in object relationships, "lone wolf," dependent on fantasy, daydreaming, or otherwise lonely modes of self-gratification or of existence. Bland in some respects but unduly and extraordinarily sensitive in others. Lofty, nebulously or abstrusely idealistic, awkward, some peculiar qualities. May be erratic or unsteady in life arrangements.

## 10. *Projective*

Suspicious, tends to give importance to proof and justification in many matters, legalistically logical; may be querulous or have chip on shoulder; generally feels easily attacked; searches out motives of others or the "real" or "hidden" reasons or meanings of things. Secretive and hiding about himself. Cautious and wary observer.

## 11. *Psychopathic*

Tends to act out his impulses, little able to foresee consequences or to anticipate the future. Gets into difficulties with law and order, shows a minimum of guilt feelings; no over-all life pattern, tries to manipulate the best out of people and situations at any given moment, may then be deferential, polite, and ingratiating; fabulizing and lying.

## 12. *Diffusion*

General lack of any more permanent character pattern. Different patterns appear on different occasions or conflicting patterns exist side by side. General unpredictability and lack of over-all integration. May appear to have no fixed attributes. May tend to drift; presence of a subjective sense of floundering and lack of commitment.

## 13. *As-if* (to be rated only as present or absent: 1, 4, or 5)

Chameleon-like "adaptiveness"; tends to assume characteristics and behavior of group he belongs to or wants to belong to.

May therefore show striking transformations and apparent integration. Lack of genuineness, depth, individuality, or originality.

### 14. *Counterphobic*

Daredevil, apparently or demonstratively fearless; feels "attack is the best defense"; appearance of superiority but constantly forced to new or repetitive feats of courage; seemingly needless exposure to frequent or constant danger.

### 15. *Depressive*

Sad, no self-confidence, pessimistic, feels unwanted, unloved, undeserving, or inferior. Little activity or outgoing striving; security-oriented, conscience-stricken. May be petulantly demanding, feeling others owe him a living, self-pitying.

### 16. *Genital* (psychosexual and psychosocial maturity)

Clear and even relationships to other people without undue ambivalence of feeling. Full reactivity to all stimuli, realistic appreciation of and responding to outside conditions as well as demands emanating from oneself. Ability to anticipate the future, delay immediate satisfaction in the interest of more certain or greater gratification in the future. Capable of full loving and of maximal, realistic utilization of own resources. Able to achieve full orgastic satisfaction. Partial drives have not necessarily disappeared but do not assume dominance; rather they manifest themselves in parts of foreplay.

## SUBJECT A

Mr. K., Age 18, Freshman, Yale College; single.
Father: Age 50, retail store owner.
Mother: Age 47, housewife.
Brother: Age 8.
Early environment: Medium-sized town in Massachusetts.
Religion: Jewish (Conservative).

The Rorschach, WAIS and TAT were administered in that order in two sessions, five days apart. We are presenting the verbatim protocol of the three tests, including scores. Bracketed statements refer to examiner verbalizations; Numbers in parentheses refer to scores.

### Wechsler Adult Intelligence Scale

*Weighted Scores and I.Q.'s*

| | | | |
|---|---|---|---|
| Information | 16 | Digit Symbol | 13 |
| Comprehension | 14 | Picture Completion | 11 |
| Arithmetic | 13 | Block Design | 17 |
| Similarities | 15 | Picture Arrangement | 13 |
| Digit Span | 12 | Object Assembly | 10 |
| Vocabulary | 14 | | |
| | Verbal IQ | 126 | |
| | Performance IQ | 119 | |
| | Total IQ | 125 | |

*Information*

1–4: not given
  5. Rubber: What do you mean—source? [Q repeated.] Rubber tree for the most part. Now synthetic (1).
  6. Presidents: Roosevelt, Eisenhower, Truman, Wilson (1).
  7. Longfellow: Poet (1).
  8. Weeks: 52 (1).
  9. Panama: Southerly (1).
  10. Brazil: South America (1).
  11. Height: About 5′ 3″ or 4″. Probably too high, though (1).
  12. Italy: Oh, I don't know. [Guess.] Rome, I suppose—maybe it is (1).
  13. Clothes: They absorb heat from the sun or from the light that falls on them (1).
  14. Washington: February 22nd (1).
  15. Hamlet: Shakespeare (1).
  16. Vatican: Center of the Catholic Religion, where the Pope resides (1).
  17. Paris: 600 miles (0).
  18. Egypt: In Asia—or is it considered Africa—between Asia and Africa. [What continent?] Well, I'll say Africa—I'm trying to picture it (1).
  19. Yeast: It breaks down—gives off $CO_2$ and alcohol from starch. Poor way to say it. The gas expands in baking (1).
  20. Population: 175 million (1).
  21. Senators: At the moment, 40—uh, two from each state—98 including Alaska (1).
  22. Genesis: Creation (1).
  23. Temperature: 100° C (1).
  24. Iliad: Homer (1).
  25. Blood vessels: White cells, red cells, uh, blood vessels? [Q repeated.] Arteries, veins, capillaries (1).
  26. Koran: Mohammedan equivalent of the Bible (1).
  27. Faust: Goethe, I think it was (1).
  28. Ethnology: Something to do with groups of people from different areas, their customs or something. [Tell me more.] Guess it's related to anthropology. I believe there's ethnic societies that have to do with these different groups of people (0).

29. Apocrypha: A collection of laws that aren't in the Bible. [Laws?] Also stories. I don't know why they're not in the Bible (0).

Raw Score: 26

*Comprehension*

1-2: not given
3. Envelope: Put it in the mailbox (2).
4. Bad Company: Well, it depends on what you consider bad company. [The conventional answer.] If you consider things they're associated with bad, then being with them will change your ideas to the point where you did some of these things. But at that point you wouldn't consider them bad [Laughs] (2).
5. Movies: I think I'd get to the nearest fire escape and while there alert everyone else—while in a position where I wouldn't get trampled (0).
6. Taxes: Having a government to rule them—the only way of living comfortably; the government can't exist without money, and this is the best way of getting money from everybody— the most honest way—not honest, but evenly distributed, you get the same from everybody (2).
7. Iron: Well, the victim of the striking—whatever striking at— when prepared for striking or completely unprepared, that's the most advantageous time to do whatever you're doing (1).
8. Child Labor: In our social system, we consider it unnecessary for children to work and cruel if they're forced to. But in some financial situations they might be forced to and there are laws to protect against this (0).
9. Forest: Well, either—the north side of a tree is supposed to have moss growing on it, which doesn't always work. If this is true, you know that the direction is north. You'd probably have some conception of the time of day. By the sun you'd know whether it was before or after noon—and know which direction is west. If not, you can always wait awhile, and see which direction it's going (2).
10. Deaf: They haven't heard—we only learn to speak by hearing spoken sounds. The best way for them to learn is to imitate what they see (2).

11. City Land: More demand for it (2).
12. Marriage: Well, so they have records of the men and so they know people are the correct ages and the like (2).
13. Brooks: People who talk a lot don't have much to back them up in the way of knowledge (1).
14. Swallow: I guess—one event—you can't judge a whole series of things just by one event—or something (2).

Raw Score: 22

*Arithmetic*

1. (1).
2. (1).
3. 1 second – $9.00 (1).
4. 1 second – four cents (1).
5. 1 second – $1.50 (1).
6. 2 seconds – 30 inches (1).
7. 1 second – 6 oranges (1).
8. 1 second – 8 hours (1).
9. 2 seconds – thirty-six cents (1).
10. 1 second –$10.50 (1).
11. 6 seconds – $3.72 [Are you sure?] Oh, thought 31¢ a can, $1.86 (0–1).
12. 1 second – $600.00 (2).
13. 10 seconds – $9.00—uh, he receives $41.00, $51.00 (2).
14. 30 seconds – Uh, yeah—that's a good one. [Laughs.] Well, 72, but I really. . . . [How did you get it?] That's a good one—I don't know. Half-a-day is $\frac{1}{12}$—and 12 × 8 is 72. No, it isn't—96. . . . Is solving arithmetic problems like that supposed to be part of my personality? Never could solve algebraic problems like this one in school (0).

Raw Score: 14

*Similarities*

1. Orange: Both fruit (2).
2. Coat: Wearing apparel (2).
3. Axe: Tools (2).
4. Dog: Animals (2).

5. North: Directions (2).
6. Eye: Parts of the body (1).
7. Air: Two states—no, that's not good. Both fluids. [Would you explain further?] Well, fluid being a state of matter. Water is a liquid, one type of a fluid (1).
8. Table: Furniture (2).
9. Egg: Concerned with life processes. [Explain further.] Well, both are the beginning of life for each particular thing (2).
10. Poem: Works of art (2).
11. Wood: Organic compounds (2).
12. Praise: They're both ways of telling a person something about themself. [Would you tell me more?] They're both evaluations of a person's doing (1).
13. Fly: Fly the noun? Nearest connection I can see is two of nature's creations (1).

Raw Score: 22

## Digit Span

Forward: 6 all on first try; failed from 7 on.
Backward: 7, failed first try on 6.

Raw Score: 13

## Vocabulary

1. Bed: Four-legged place where one sleeps (2).
2. Ship: Ocean vessel (2).
3. Penny: Piece of money (2).
4. Winter: Season, cold season (2).
5. Repair: Fix (2).
6. Breakfast: First meal of the day (2).
7. Fabric: Cloth (2).
8. Slice: Cut—into thin pieces (2).
9. Assemble: Put together in orderly fashion (2).
10. Conceal: Hide (2).
11. Enormous: Very large (2).
12. Hasten: Quicken the pace (2).
13. Sentence: Group of words expressing a complete thought (2).
14. Regulate: To control the rate (2).

15. Commence: Begin (2).
16. Ponder: Think (2).
17. Cavern: A large room-like cavity (1).
18. Designate: Point out (2).
19. Domestic: Pertaining to home (2).
20. Consume: Devour (2).
21. Terminate: Put to an end (2).
22. Obstruct: Hold up the completion of an action (1).
23. Remorse: Grief—not, well . . . nostalgia. [Would you explain further?] Thinking back over a particular thing and feeling sorry that it happened, expressing grief that it happened. One might live with remorse, having gone to a meeting when he might have been better off some place else [Laughs] (1).
24. Sanctuary: Place of protection (2).
25. Matchless: Without a match. Don't think I ever heard the word. Match meaning . . . putting two corresponding things together—people (0).
26. Reluctant: Hesitant (2).
27. Calamity: Disaster (2).
28. Fortitude: Strength (2).
29. Tranquil: Quiet (2).
30. Edifice: Great structure. [Structure?] For instance, a monument (2).
31. Compassion: [Pause] Liking for something or somebody. [Would you tell me more?] What one might feel towards a loved one (0).
32. Tangible: Something one can put his hands on, material (2).
33. Perimeter: The edge (1).
34. Audacious: Bold (2).
35. Ominous: Foreboding (2).
36. Tirade: I don't think I could explain that—I mean I don't think I know the definition of that (0).
37. Encumber: Is that to burden? (2).
38. Plagiarize: To copy (1).
39. Impale: To kill by a sharp object, piercing (1).
40. Travesty: Not sure of that one either. [Take a guess.] I don't think I could. Might be able to recognize it in usage, but . . . (0).

Raw Score: 66

*Digit Symbol*

All correct.                                    Raw Score: 67

*Picture Completion*

1. Door: 1 second – Knob (1).
2. Pig: 1 second – Tail (1).
3. Girl: 1 second – Nose (1).
4. Car: 1 second – Handles (1).
5. Card: 2 seconds – Diamond (1).
6. Pitcher: 1 second – Water (1).
7. Glasses: 1 second – Bridge (1).
8. Violin: 4 seconds – Key . . . I think you call it (1).
9. Boat: 1 second – Person rowing. [What's most important?] Oh, oarlock (0–1).
10. Bulb: 4 seconds – Threads (1).
11. Flag: 19 seconds – Thirty-five stars only (1).
12. Man, Dog: 3 seconds – The dog isn't sunk in the snow. [What is it that is missing?] Oh, these are, I take it, indentations. [Explain further.] The dog is not so light that it wouldn't go below the surface in a footstep. [Prints?] More than that—it would be sunk in, too (0–1).
13. Map: 2 seconds – Florida (1).
14. Ship: 2 seconds – Smokestacks (1).
15. Crab: 7 seconds – Leg (1).
16. Vanity: 3 seconds – Reflection of arm (1).
17. Man: 8 seconds – Small finger on left hand (1).
18. Sun: 28 seconds – I can't see anything specific missing other than the tree looks alone. Oh, the man's shadow (0–1).
19. Horse: 32 seconds – I don't see anything (0).
20. Woodpile: 16 seconds – Snow on the logs (1).
21. Girl: 36 seconds – I don't see anything—the ear is covered by hair, but it might be that (0).

Raw Score: 16–19

*Block Designs*

1. 4 seconds – Correct (4).
2. 3 seconds – Correct (4).

3. 5 seconds – Correct (4).
4. 9 seconds – Correct (4).
5. 9 seconds – Correct (4).
6. 13 seconds – Correct (4).
7. 22 seconds – Correct (6).
8. 33 seconds – Correct [Slight inefficiency, some awkwardness in placing blocks] (6).
9. 54 seconds – Correct (6).
10. 35 seconds – Correct (6).
   After completion of 10, asked: "Did I do average on that one?" [Faster than average.]

Raw Score: 48

### Picture Arrangement

1. Nest: 2 seconds – WXY (4).
2. House: 2 seconds – PAT [Subject is very involved, goes as fast as possible] (4).
3. Hold up: 4 seconds – ABCD (4).
4. Comic Book: 12 seconds – CATOMI. [Tell me the story.] He's walking along. Two children start fighting over a comic book. He's the great pacifier, makes them become friends again. After they're friends again, they forget about comics (0).
5. Door: 17 seconds – OPENS (4).
6. Flirt: 19 seconds – JANET (4).
7. Fish: 17 seconds – EFGHIJ. [Tell me the story.] He was fishing, he caught some fish, then another. A partner of his is down with a diving suit, and comes up—he had been putting the fish on the line (6).
8. Taxi: 41 seconds – SAMUEL. [Tell me the story.] A man with a statue—a store model—hails a taxi. He is sitting with the model. He looks around, realizes it looks like he's sitting very close to a girl there in back. Embarrassed, he pushes the model over (4).

Raw Score: 30

### Object Assembly

1. Manikin: 14 seconds – [Head, legs, arms—going very fast, has trouble fitting arms and legs exactly] (7).

2. Profile: 49 seconds – [Ear upside down—corrects it spontaneously] (9).
3. Hand: 57 seconds – [First tries thumb alongside hand] (7).
4. Elephant: 44 seconds – [Rump wrong—corrects it spontaneously] (10).

Raw Score: 33

## Rorschach Test

This test was administered and scored in the Rapaport-Schafer manner. Inquiry was carried out after each card, following the free association. In the protocol presented, italicized statements in brackets refer to inquiries made after each response.

*Card I. Reaction time: 10 seconds. Total time: 3 minutes.*

1. Well, yeah. [Laughs.] I guess some sort of insect of some type—at least the body. Wings are sort of—wouldn't fit in with insect, but. . . . [*What made it look like an insect?*] Well, three body parts like insects—head, thorax, abdomen. Plus three pairs of things that led out from body that might be the beginning of legs. Also, head with two things sticking out that might be mouth parts or something. [*Anything else?*] No. [Center D.] Want me to go deeper? [*Up to you.*]
2. Well, somehow the outsides—can't say what they would be. But center could be an insect or the figure of a woman with her hands up in the air, I imagine. [*What made it look like a woman?*] Just standing there . . . the shape. Actually I still can't see anything in the wings or outermost things. [Laughs.] Is it all right to hold it upside down? [*Up to you.*] It just looks like the same thing upside down. That's it.
Scores: 1: D (Do tend) F + A. 2: D M + H P.

*Card II. Reaction time: 25 seconds. Total time: 3 minutes, 30 seconds.*

1. Well, uh—I think—as far as the separate sections, this bottom part looks like the exact replica of some butterfly I've seen—that's the bottom red part. [*What made it look like a butterfly?*] Well, as far as I can remember it's the exact shape—

don't remember which kind—swallow-tail, I think. Scalloped wings and little tail-like things, just as on the butterfly. [*Anything else?*] No, I think that's the major thing. The coloring was very different than on any butterfly. [*Coloring different?*] I've never seen a butterfly that color.

2. I guess the big dark blotches would be some kind of animal. I think I could show you. Up to this point where it's darker, could be sheep [shows]. Not where it's lighter gray, but up to that point. [*What made it look like a sheep?*] Well, it seems to be—looks like some type of an animal, and I think a sheep's head is the same shape as the head on it. Could also be a dog, but it seemed the same shape as a sheep.

3. The top parts, I don't know—let's see. [Laughs.] I can't think of any logical thing for the top parts. . . . Well, I can't see anything that I can actually convince myself that it looks like that. Might have the shape of a butterfly with its wings closed, but it doesn't actually. [*What made it look like a butterfly?*] Well, it isn't actually the shape, but the closest thing I could come to if I had to name it. I think that's it.

Scores: 1: D F + A P.   2: D (Do tend) F + Ad.
3: D F ± A.

*Card III. Reaction time: 30 seconds. Total time: 4 minutes, 15 seconds.*

1. Well, I imagine these dark shapes—some types of people —they're disjointed at the waist, but in general they're like people. The feet and hands are—I don't know—like some sort of reptilian feet, I think—webbed, or something to that effect. [*Describe the people.*] Well, rather odd looking—I think their joints are bent at rather odd angles. Their heads were rather pointed at the top—where the mouth would be. Uh—also disjointed at the waist with odd looking hands and feet.

2. Let's see. I think the little red things at the top—at each corner—possibly like the very young sprout of a plant of some sort. Top roots were broken off after being pulled out—something to that effect. [*What made it look like a sprout?*] Well, mainly the end of the stem with minute points coming off the top of it that reminded me of roots coming off right near the stem.

3. I guess the thing in the center—best thing I could say would be some kind of ragged, sloppy bow tie. [*Ragged and sloppy?*] The edges being not smooth, regular. [*What about it looking like a bow tie?*] The center part seemed to run—uh—well, separate, slightly bulged like the shape of a knot. The edges are sort of triangular. I think that's it.

Scores: 1: D FM + H P.    2: D F ∓ Pl.    3: D F + Cg P.

*Card IV. Reaction time: 45 seconds. Total time: 3 minutes, 7 seconds.*

1. Uh, well . . . I think the darker shape which takes up most of the area appears to be one of those flying squirrels or something. The head looks like the head of a squirrel from above. Also four appendages and membrane is stretched between the four appendages that a flying squirrel would have on each side for gliding. [*What made it look like a membrane?*] Well, it gave the general impression of a squirrel. And the four legs weren't easily distinguishable as legs, but sort of connected, just like the membrane on a flying squirrel. [*Anything else that made it look like a membrane?*] No, just that, I guess. [Subject indicates location: First includes "tail," then doesn't, then does. Comments, "It looks disconnected."]

2. And down at the bottom—two appendages—one on either side—that part looks like some kind of a boot—just considering that. That's about all I can make out of that.

Scores: 1: W F (C) ± A.    2: D F + Cg P.

*Card V. Reaction time: 40 seconds. Total time: 3 minutes, 12 seconds.*

1. Well, uh [Sighs]. . . . Well, in general, leaving off the very top and bottom and a little bit of each end, it reminds me of a kind of pastry—I don't know what you call it. Made by rolling dough around—sort of appears to have the joints in it. [*What made it look like pastry?*] Well, it's just, I guess, the right shape. Well, looks like the shadow thrown by a piece of pastry. The outlines and little bumps look just like pastry. Just this particular piece of pastry that comes to my mind. [*What do you mean, out-*

*lines and bumps?*] Well, some sort of sugar or something to that effect on the outside of this. So if there were a shadow, it would appear as bumps on the edges. [*How do you mean shadow?*] I guess just the coloring, the lack of three dimensions. [*Lack of three dimensions?*] Well, it takes up most of the area of this ink-blot—and this would be just about the size of this piece of pastry —the three dimensions would be evident in the pastry, I mean.

2. At the very top, there's a sort of—oh, I guess what you'd call a head in the shadows where the grays are differentiated. Round at the top, something like an ear over there. As far as I can see, everything else seems superfluous.

Scores: 1: Dr F ± Food.   2: Dr F (C) ± Hd.

*Card VI. Reaction time: 20 seconds. Total time: 3 minutes, 8 seconds.*

1. Well, the top sort of looks like—er—the beginning of a violin—the handle, the part you hold, which is long and then widens out into the violin. Not the complete violin—just that much. [Top D.] There's two little things that might be the little things you tighten the strings with. I don't think I can make anything out of the other—the bottom half. I think maybe I can.

2. Part of it looks like an old typewriter or a desk typewriter, where the part that holds the keys sticks out a little bit and the other part goes straight up. It's a little vague. [Side D.] [*What made it look like a typewriter?*] I know we used to have an old typewriter—old fashioned. One part where the keys were extended out toward you—the other part went straight up. And part of this seemed to fit that. I think that's it.

Scores: 1: D (Do tend) F + Obj.   2: Dr F − Obj.

*Card VII. Reaction time: 25 seconds. Total time: 2 minutes, 16 seconds.*

1. I think each side of the top part of this looks like a puppy of some sort, with the tail stuck out and the ears up. [*What gave you the impression of a puppy?*] Well, sort of young looking—it looked sort of small. I guess the body was small. Just

generally young looking. I don't know—they seem to be balanced on something or other, but I don't know what it might be. I think that's it.

Score: D F ± A.

*Card VIII. Reaction time: 25 seconds. Total time: 4 minutes, 45 seconds.*

1. Well, on either edge, looking at this sideways, there appears to be some kind of animal—I can't really place the animal. I can see four legs, head, and body. In the place where you usually see a tail there doesn't appear to be one. But I can see sort of the stump. Holding it this way, it appears to be climbing on something. Also, it looks like fur on it because of the unevenness of the edges. Actually, nothing else makes much sense.

2. Possibly in the middle, darker blue objects look like some sort of pillows with trilled edges. They have sort of a roundish, plump look to them. [*What makes them look roundish, plump?*] Just sort of appeared to be wrinkles, indentations in the center, as though you pushed in part of them. I guess the shading. [*Pillows?*] Well, just the general shape and the fact that they were sort of plump looking.

3. I think one little place right in the center might look like one little bone of a fish—spine—with little bones coming off of it—little fine bones.

4. At the bottom, although the shapes don't look like them, the colors look like sherbet—also the texture—maybe orange, strawberry, something to that effect.

Scores: 1: D F + A P. 2: D F (C) ± Obj. 3: Dr F + At. 4: D C (C) Food.

*Card IX.*

1. I don't think I can make anything out of this [1 minute, 30 seconds]. [Shakes head: 2 minutes]. I actually can't see anything in it—and also I would say it doesn't even look like an inkblot [2 minutes, 30 seconds]. I can't see a thing in it.

Score: Fail

*Card X. Reaction time: 40 seconds. Total time: 6 minutes, 22 seconds.*

1. I think the blue shapes on the outside—discounting the color—look like some sort of algae, seaweed of some sort. Not stringy, but a ripped appearance like a piece of lettuce, or something to that effect.

2. The large long red objects—vaguely reminiscent of the state of California, the shape of the state, that is.

3. I think the gray thing at the top—part of it—looks like the long stem of a plant.

4. Right next to it, plants like clovers with long stems and little leaves at the top.

5. Down at the bottom—the green things look like some sort of caterpillars. [*What made them look like caterpillars?*] Sort of the right color—and long and thin.

6. In the very center towards the top—that little yellow thing —recalls to my mind some sort of experiment where they take two tubes to represent lungs and have some sort of pipe branching off of this. This is to demonstrate breathing.

7. And at the bottom—the two yellow things near the center —appear to be some kind of dog—I think a collie—with its rear feet—hind feet, I mean, stretched out. This could also be in front of a building—they both appear to be looking toward each other. [*What made it look like a collie?*] Just the long snout and it appears to be a big dog with a large body. [*What gave you the impression of a large body?*] The body part I consider large in relationship to the head. [*You mentioned they could be in front of a building.*] Bronx Zoo—has two statues of lions—these look like them since they're symmetrical and are facing each other. That's all.

Scores: 1: D F ∓ Pl Food.    2: D F ∓ Geog.    3: Dr F ± Pl. 4: Dr F ± Pl.  5: D FC + A.  6: D F + At Fab.  7: D F + A P Fab.

*Card IX, repeated. Reaction time: 1 minute. Total time: 3 minutes, 55 seconds.*

1. Well, stretching a point. The center light greenish thing that seems to fade off—the part where you can see light through

—well, that reminds me of sand dollars. They're sort of a lightish shade with little cut-out holes. [*Light shade?*] Well, a sand dollar is light gray. This is a greenish shade—but nevertheless it has little color and is sort of gray and smooth.

2. At the very top, the orange on the two sides appears to be bridged by fine lines. This could be the top of a sphere, with an eclipse of the sun, prominences coming off of it—pieces of gas thrown off from the sun. [*What made it look like the top of a sphere with an eclipse of the sun?*] Lines from either side are curved—that's the edge of the sphere. Just the color and the way these lines were shooting away from this reminded me of the prominences. Most of the other things—I just don't see anything.

Scores: 1: Add. Drs (C) F A. 2: Dr CF Na. De F ± Sphere Eclipse Fab. Comb.

## Summary of Rorschach Scores

| | | | | | | |
|---|---|---|---|---|---|---|
| W | 1 | | F + 11 | | A | 8 |
| D | 19 | | F − 1 | | Ad | 1 |
| Dr | 6 | | F ± 4 | | H | 2 |
| (Do tendency 3) | | | F ∓ 3 | | Hd | 1 |
| | | | M + 1 | | Obj | 3 |
| Qualitative | | | FM + 1 | | Clg | 2 |
| Fab. | | 2 | FC + 1 | | Pl | 4 |
| Aut. Logic tend. | | 1 | C(C) | 1 | Geog | 1 |
| | | | F(C) ± 3 | | At | 2 |
| | | | | | Food | 2 (1 add.) |
| W per cent | | 4 | R | 26 | EB | 1.5–2 |
| D per cent | | 73 | F per cent | 76–96 | A per cent | 33 |
| Dr per cent | | 23 | F + per cent | 79–84 | H per cent | 11 |
| | | | | | P | 7 |

*Failure: Card IX* (Readministered at end of test)

Additional: 1: Drs (C)F A   2: Dr CF Nat   3: Dr F ± Sphere Fab Comb 1.

**Thematic Apperception Test**

We used 14 pictures, 12 of which are commonly administered; the Picasso and the Line Drawing cards, part of the original Harvard series, are generally not used. We have found both cards useful for eliciting rich material as part of our clinical battery and so have included them here.

*Card 1* (Boy with violin)

May I start off with the characters themselves? Well, there's a young boy contemplating his broken violin. Possibly he was told to practice his violin and was left alone, but got carried away and maybe went out to play and took it along with him. During his play an accident happened to it and it got broken. He's probably now deciding some way to repair it. Probably also thinking about the punishment he might get because of his not obeying. That's about it. [*Ultimate outcome?*] That's it. Uh, probably he won't succeed in getting it repaired in too great a condition I would imagine, depending on the cost or value of the instrument, his punishment will vary with that. If it's fairly expensive—I don't know how much violins are—he'll have to do certain chores to make up for his mistakes. [*Feel?*] He probably realizes he didn't obey and the whole incident happened because of that and might have been avoided. [*Whom didn't he obey?*] One of his parents—probably his mother—who might be more connected with his practicing on the instrument.

*Card 3 BM* (Figure on floor by a couch)

May I ask if that is a gun? Guess it is. Well, this woman might have come to a friend's house on a call from the friend that the friend might have needed help in some way. And arriving, she has found the friend shot, presumably by herself—the friend's self. She's terror-stricken or grief-stricken and starts crying because of the idea that her friend is dead. She probably will soon call the police. I would imagine that she has already ascertained that the friend is dead. Because if she found the friend still living, I'm quite sure she would have called the hospital first. I think that's all.

### Card 4 (Young woman and man)

Well, this looks like either a husband and wife, or a boy and girl friend. Possibly he's been angered to a great extent by someone. And is now intent upon seeking revenge in some manner. The woman, who is much calmer and probably using better judgment, realizes that it would be much wiser for him to let it ride for the moment. Probably because the man appears very uncontrollable. He will end up by doing what he wants and not listening to the woman. [*Angered by what?*] The man in the picture might in some way be connected with some type of gangsters who have—because they were powerful—thus far controlled his life to a great extent. But in this fit of anger, he feels that he can break the ties with them.

### Card 15 (Old man in graveyard)

This man looks like a character out of an Edgar Allan Poe story. I don't think—I might be able to make up a story in this fashion, because this is what it looks like to me. However, being more realistic, I'd say this is just an old man whose wife or very close companion has just died—recently died. Or perhaps he is just going back to visit the grave of a long-deceased friend. He's probably rather lonely because of his age and that's probably what prompted him to go to the graveyard. At the moment, he's probably standing, reviewing events connected with him and this person in his mind. I couldn't really say what the outcome would be. Probably he would just go back to his normal life immediately after this incident. But the memory of this person would still be fresh in his mind.

### Card 5 (Woman in doorway)

Well, this woman possibly was in a different room in the house, might have heard a noise and come to this room to investigate, since that's where the noise sounded. On opening the door she's quite surprised to find that it was only a pet dog or a cat—of hers. Probably she'll just bring the cat to another room, or where it's usually kept. I think that's all. [*How did she feel when she heard the noise?*] I think that would probably depend on many external factors. For the sake of the story, she was startled with the sudden noise. It probably didn't occur to her that it might be something like a cat or animal. Probably this happened quite suddenly and she didn't stop to think what it was. Had there been anybody else in the house, she might have thought it was them and come to see if they needed help in any way.

*Card 6 BM* (Old woman looking away from young man)

This looks like a man and his mother. He's probably been away from the house deciding things, and has just told her that he is leaving to move far away. He knows that she will probably feel lonely and he, therefore, doesn't know exactly how to tell her this and feels about having to—poorly. This probably came as a surprise to her, although she might have thought this would happen sooner or later. As far as the outcome, most likely she'll just have to accept this. [*Why did he decide to leave?*] Could be for any number of reasons. He might have been offered a job in some distant city.

*Card 7 BM* (Older man looking at younger man)

Well, this might be a young man—who's discussing something with an older man—possibly just a friend. He might have needed advice as far as . . . [pause] well, as far as business or perhaps relations with some mutual friend. Probably the older man might give him some advice or point out the solution indirectly, since he is probably a good deal wiser in such matters.

*Card 8 BM* (Operation scene)

This young boy might have been kidnaped by the man lying on the bed. He probably struggled with the man who was holding a gun—rifle—and accidentally the gun went off. The man was shot in the stomach. The boy felt guilty, even towards this person who tried to harm him, and immediately summoned aid. Since this was a serious wound, the doctors have decided to remove the bullet on the spot, rather than removing him to the hospital. In the picture, the boy is probably thinking about the events which have just occurred. Probably if the man were shot in the stomach, the outcome will be that he will die, thus receiving his punishment for kidnaping. [*Why does the boy feel guilty?*] For causing the man to be shot.

### Card 10 (Heads of embracing couple)

This might be a brother of a recently deceased husband with the widow. Being very greatly affected by her husband's death, she has come to see the brother. She probably just needed to express her sorrow to someone and is now crying. The brother kisses her on the forehead and tells her everything will be all right, will work out for the best. She'll probably return home much more contented. Period.

### Line Drawing (Old man on shoulders of another old man)

I wouldn't say this is a realistic picture. But it seems to represent the older generation trying to explain that the—their old laws of human behavior—proper human behavior—should still be in effect, and that there should be no more fighting individually or in mass. Probably explaining that they're older and wiser. That's all. [*Ultimate outcome?*] Probably it won't do any good if history does repeat itself. [*Explaining this to whom?*] The younger generation.

### Card 12 M (Hypnosis scene)

This looks like an event in past times with a doctor who has the belief that he can cure this woman of her ailments by using hypnosis. Since she was suffering, though she didn't believe in this, she consented, and is now being hypnotized. On awakening, she might have had it imprinted on her mind that she will feel well. And will probably go on thinking that she is well until some new ailment arises. [*What sort of ailment?*] Some physical —aches and pains in general. Something she doesn't understand herself. [Looks at his watch.]

*Card 13 MF* (Woman on bed with man standing)

Well, this looks like a somewhat elderly man, as far as I can tell from the white hair. He has probably come to see his daughter and found that she has not kept his high ideals and lives in a somewhat barren apartment. Probably earning money as a prostitute. He can't bear to look at his daughter, of whom he was once proud. Probably will leave and not make any attempt to contact her again.

*Picasso* (Nude couple; older woman with infant)

[Sighs.] Well, this looks possibly like the mother of the daughter who is holding the child of the daughter and her . . . and I guess we might say friend. Uh—she—will not—uh—permit them to keep the child, care for the child, which was born out of wedlock. It appears that possibly the couple have decided to marry and would like custody of the child. The—well, as far as what is correct, the girl actually should take charge of her own child, and the outcome will probably be thus. [*Mother?*] Well, she'll probably give up the child to the daughter because she will realize that that's correct—that's my opinion.

*Card 16* (Blank card)

Well, this looks like an overhead view of Oswego, N.Y., not quite sure of the name—in December after their snowfall of 7 inches—uh—7 feet. This is a baseball field as it looked the day after—[Smiles]. [*Can you make up story?*] Well, at the moment, beneath the scene pictured, there's a couple of tunnels with some children who are playing in the snow and have found out that it's very pleasant and warm underneath all that snow. Probably their fun in the snow will be short-lived, as their parents on missing them will retrieve them, as it would be dangerous in case of a snowslide or the snow piling up on top of them so they were trapped. This will probably remain for a long time in their minds, as I doubt whether this happens too often. That's it.

## DISCUSSION OF RATINGS

### A. Ideational Styles

#### 1. *Cognitive reactivity*, Rating: 2

The subject is rather blocked on all tests. On the Rorschach he gives 26 responses and fails Card IX. His reaction time is slow, averaging 30 seconds to the first response on each Rorschach card. He is not fluent and is doubtful and circumstantial (1 minute 10 seconds per Rorschach response). On the Information subtest he responds to the question: "What is the capital of Italy?" with: "Oh, I don't know," [*guess*] "Rome, I suppose, maybe it is." His responsiveness to the TAT is very limited, his stories are brief and frequently require further questioning. He cannot be considered as spontaneous and fluent as a rating of 3 would reflect, but he is not as meager in his reactions as a rating of 1 would indicate.

#### 2. *Originality*, Rating: $2_{4.5}$

The whole realm of ideas expressed in the tests is not particularly unique or original. The TAT stories are basically bland, but on occasion they deviate strikingly from the standard formula, as on Cards 1, 8 BM and 13 MF. The subject gives commonplace responses to the Rorschach, but, as on the TAT, many have an unusual twist and are quite idiosyncratic. On Card III of the Rorschach (top, side red areas) he responds as follows: "It's like a very young sprout—a plant. The top, the roots were broken off." On the same card he describes the "bow tie" as being ragged and sloppy. On Card V his "pastry" response is altogether unusual and rare, particularly with the elaboration of the shadow. On the WAIS there is no expression of a high degree of originality, although an occasional nuance is in evidence (e.g., he defines "bed" as a "four legged place where one sleeps"). The main rating of 2 refers to the mediocre degree of originality evidenced on the whole, whereas the subscore of 4.5 is based on the occasional unusual twist.

3. *Abstractness,* Rating: 2.5

His over-all IQ of 125 and his verbal IQ of 126 imply a good potential capacity for abstractness in relation to the average population. However, compared to other Yale freshmen he shows himself less than appropriately abstract. On the Rorschach his W per cent is 4, he has only 1½ M's and there are no signs of a really good integrative effort. On the TAT, Cards 8 BM, 16, and the Line Drawing call for stories emphasizing the abstract, yet no such trend is in evidence. On the WAIS his Block Design and Similarities scores are high and the content of his responses on the Similarities subtest shows a parsimonious and appropriately abstract approach. It appears that when confronted with purely formal, impersonal problems he can function abstractly. In more personally oriented and affectively toned problem situations, his mode of response is more circumstantial and concretistic. In general then his position seems to be between the ratings of 2 and 3.

4. *Lability,* Rating: 3.5

There is a marked dryness particularly in situations where affects or emotions should influence his functioning. Color responsivity on the Rorschach is fairly minimal; he has one FC, one C(C), and he fails Card IX. The FC on Card X is a caterpillar, a weak color response. He does not seem to be much swayed by impulse, although there is some expression of affect in such contents as "a young sprout." The fact that a C combined with shading appears on the Rorschach seems quite remarkable; the shading may well stand for some anxiety and inhibition in relation to affect. One might speculate that more affective behavior may develop either in specific stress situations or at some time in the future when controls are somewhat loosened. When confronted by affect-laden stimuli on the TAT he expresses little lability, but tends to become hypercontrolled and overly rationalistic. His WAIS responses are quite steady throughout; only when confronted with failure does he express some excitement as on item 14 on the Arithmetic subtest.

### 5. *Attentiveness*, Rating: 2

The subject seems to be a fairly hyperalert person. His Dr per cent on the Rorschach is 23 as compared with a W per cent of 4. His very first response on the Rorschach, to Card I, already shows a preoccupation with minor detail. In the inquiry he approaches the task in the same manner: ". . . three body parts like insect head, thorax, abdomen, plus three pairs of things that let out from the body that might be the beginning of legs. And also a head with two things sticking out." On Card VI he sees "the beginning of a violin," also a typewriter "where the part that holds the keys sticks out a little bit and the other part goes straight up." On the TAT the presence of hyperalertness and of active avoidance is noted. On 3 BM, for example, he immediately asks about the item on the floor and the examiner noted that the subject watched him writing and paced his words to the speed of that writing very carefully. The WAIS does not indicate significant hyperalertness; Picture Completion is one of the lower scores, Arithmetic is not particularly high and nothing in the content implies heightened attentiveness. Again, the more objective and impersonal the test, the less expression of attention to small detail is in evidence.

### B. Prominent Affects

### 1. *Depression*, Rating: 3.5

A number of themes in the TAT involve loneliness, people leaving, being isolated, unable to get better, dying, and death itself; and people functioning at a relatively low social and moral level (3 BM, 6, 8 BM, 10, 12 M, 13 MF, 15, Picasso). In the Rorschach there is a very strong oral emphasis; "the pastry" on Card V and the "sherbet" on Card IX are noteworthy. The "shadow" of the "pastry" response has an especially depressive tone since it implies that the fantasied oral supplies are not available. There are also the "uprooted plant," the "ragged bow tie" on Card III, and the "ripped lettuce" on Card X. The three F(C)'s further reflect his interest in dark color and shading. He fails Card IX, modulated color responsivity is limited to one FC, and he has only one W. The WAIS performance, too, points to mild feelings of inadequacy and worthlessness; after explaining the

"Yeast" question in the Information subtest he states: "Poor way to say it." On item 18 of Picture Completion he responds ". . . the tree looks alone." Neither the Verbal-Performance IQ differential nor the variation of subtest scores are, on the other hand, indicative of noteworthy depression. If one were to rate dynamic aspects of depression rather than the experienced and expressed affect the rating would be near 4.5. However, his experience and expression of this affect seem markedly limited.

### 2. Guilt, Rating: 4

Five stories in the TAT seem to reflect rather clearly the subject's feelings of guilt—to Cards 1, 3 BM, 8 BM, 13 MF, and the Picasso picture. On 3 BM the friend did not manage to get there in time to save the heroine and there is also a slip: "On arriving he had found the friend shot, presumably by herself," which he quickly corrects to "the friend's self." Here, it is as if the subject thinks some aggressive impulse might get out of control; this appears to be an exaggeration of how one might feel under the influence of guilt. On 8 BM the boy experiences guilt after he shoots a kidnaper who then dies. The boy feels guilty even though this person tried to harm him. Furthermore, the kidnaper was shot accidentally in the struggle. The subject also shows a marked tendency to put disorderly situations quickly back in order; as evidenced, for instance, in his story to the Picasso picture. The lover becomes a friend, which makes the situation more acceptable, and the people get married after having obviously had an indecent affair. On Card 13 MF the elderly man finds his daughter has not kept his high ideals and that she is earning money as a prostitute: "He will leave and will not make any attempt to contact her again." This implies a great deal of moral harshness which is likely to go together with considerable guilt.

### 3. Affection and love, Rating: 2

On the Rorschach there is little indication of interpersonal warmth; there is only 1 FC, 2 H's, and 1 Hd. None of the three human responses is expressed in an easy manner and without equivocation. On Card I it is "an insect or the figure of a woman," on Card III he responds: "These dark shapes—some types of people—they are disjointed at the waist, but in general like people. The feet and hands are—I don't know—like some sort of reptilian feet. . . ." On Card V the Hd is verbalized as follows: ". . . oh, I guess what you'd call a head in the shadows . . . something like an ear over there." On two of his TAT stories there are themes reflecting affection. On Card 10 the brother comforts the widow and she goes away relieved, that is, the brother gives the widow affection. The other story, which is much more infantile and has less to do with the real giving of affection, is Card 16 (the blank card) where a cheerful situation of children playing under the snow is described. Most of the stories, however, are in terms of aggression or morality or involve sad occasions, On Card 13 MF, for instance, the father has the chance to give affection and support to his misguided daughter, but instead cannot look at her and leaves. Also on Card 6 BM of the TAT there is no expression of feelings when the man tells his mother that he is leaving and he is aware she will probably feel lonely. From all this we may infer rather little capacity on the subject's part for accepting loving feelings within himself.

### 4. Shame, Rating: X (cannot say)

No rating was given because it seems impossible to distinguish between experienced and/or expressed feelings of shame in the subject and a more basic sense of shame of which he may not be aware. Relevant in his responses may be the disjointedness of people and the separation of the lower part from the upper part of the body on the Rorschach. In the TAT he completely avoids talking about the nakedness of the people on the Picasso card or the exposure of the woman on 13 MF.

### 5. Frustration and thwartedness, dissatisfaction, Rating: 4

On the Rorschach, figures are described as disjointed; the "little sprout" on Card III is "pulled out" so it cannot grow any further; the "pastry" on Card V is only a shadow. On Card VIII he responds with ". . . possibly the middle, the dark blue objects look like some sort of pillows with trilled edges. They have a round, plump look to them." When asked in the inquiry about the "roundish and plump" he states that there appear to be "wrinkles and indentations" in the center as though "pushed in." Things seeming originally good, like the "pastry" and the "plump round pillows" (very likely symbolic representations of breasts), become "shadows" or are "wrinkled and pushed in"; in either case they provide no source of nourishment. On the TAT there is a considerable expression of relevant feelings. On Card 1 the violin is broken in an accident and the hero's punishment will vary depending on the cost or value of the instrument. On 3 BM a friend is killed in a strange way; on Card 4 someone is angered, but cannot express it; on 13 MF there is the frustration and thwartedness of the father with his prostitute daughter, and on 15 the subject talks about loneliness. He also seems to have a sense of thwartedness in connection with his work, frequently opposing affection and work in a way that implies that one must not allow affection to stand in the way of work; this is best represented in the "violin" and the "mother-son" stories. There are, however, a few stories such as the one on 7 BM in which somebody wiser can help him solve certain problems.

### 6. *Elation,* Rating: 1.5

Nowhere in the record is there any noteworthy indication of elation. The only expressions of joyfulness, although on an infantile level, appear on Card 16 of the TAT; also on the Block Design, Picture Arrangement, and Object Assembly subtests of the WAIS the subject became very much involved and worked at a rapid pace. In most cases, when something of an elated flavor appears in the record, especially in the Rorschach, it is rapidly altered into a negative, unpleasant image, such as the previously mentioned "pillow" and "pastry."

### 7. *Anxiety,* Rating: 3

On the Rorschach the subject produced 7 Dr's and only 1W response, and except for the pure F scores his largest number of determinants are in the F(C) category. In addition, the style of language (e.g. Card I, 1: "Well, yeah [laughs] I guess some sort of insect of some type, at least the body. Wings are sort of—wouldn't fit in with insect, but" [long pause], and the content (e.g., Card II, 2: ". . . there's a sort of—oh I guess what you'd call a head in the shadows . . .") point to the presence of moderate anxiety. In terms of formal quality his responses are good (F + percent 85–96). The WAIS shows a drop in Digit Span and Arithmetic, but on the whole it is quite orderly. In the TAT anxiety is reflected both in form and content of the stories, but the subject does not present a picture of a person overwrought by anxiety. There are more expressions, perhaps, of superego-anxiety in concerns over being wrong, than of anxiety related to feelings of being overwhelmed by impulses.

### 8. *Hostility*, Rating: 3

On the whole we find a moderate amount of expressed and/or experienced hostility, although the subject's potential for it appears to be much higher. On the TAT, hostility is expressed in terms of punishment (Card 1), of having things broken, of shooting people on Cards 3 BM and 8 BM; and in response to the Line Drawing he states that there should be no more fighting. He appears to be conscious of a good deal of hostility, otherwise the aggressive themes on the TAT would probably be expressed in more disguised ways. Rejection of hostile impulses often comes only after they have entered consciousness and appear as possible ways to behave; only at that point the subject's ego allies itself with control (see item 4 of Picture Arrangement on the WAIS). Less directly expressed hostility is represented by the "ripping," the "tearing," and the "stumps" that occur on the Rorschach. If hostility were rated in terms of its underlying presence and without regard to his experience or expression of it, he would receive a rating of 4.

### C. Prominent Defenses

### 1. *Repression*, Rating: 2.5

Repression is not one of his major defenses. On the Rorschach there is only one FC and one C(C); he fails Card IX, exhibits a lack of sponteneity, and his expression of affect or fantasy is on the whole quite limited. While the Rorschach findings point to a moderate repressive trend, his functioning on the WAIS does not bear it out. His verbal IQ of 126 is seven points above his performance IQ; also, his Information subscore is higher than his Comprehension subscore, another indication that repression is not heavily relied upon. There is no extensive blocking on the TAT and affective reactions only rarely intrude into the flow of the stories.

### 2. Denial, Rating: 2

Denial is generally undistinguished and in this subject's case is not a major defense. Denial implies a degree of active transformation of manifestations of impulse or representations of reality. Of this he shows relatively little. Painful and aggressive themes in the TAT stories come through clearly although without much elaboration; the active element in denial is clearly missing.

### 3. Projection, Rating: 3.5

On the Rorschach there is a heavy emphasis on Dr (23 per cent) and four responses fall into the "object" category. The contents of some of the responses have a highly idiosyncratic though not a bizarre flavor, e.g., the "pastry" (Card V), the "pillows" (Card VIII), the "lung experiment" and the "State of California" on Card X, the "eclipse," "the prominence and sphere of the sun" on readministered Card IX. These responses do not so much represent a breaking through of primary process thought into an overwhelmed ego as, much more, a kind of active putting out of some rather idiosyncratic percepts. On the TAT there is evidence of projection on 3 BM: ". . . on arriving he found the friend shot, presumably by herself—the friend's self . . ." and in the story on card 4 where gangsters control the hero's life.

### 4. Reaction formation, Rating: 1.5

This defense is quite undistinguished in this subject's test records, where we find no conspicuous concern with orderliness or cleanliness, and little or no concern with tenderness. On the other hand, there are no expressions of open slovenly or smutty patterns, either.

## 5. *Isolation,* Rating: 4

We have already described his heavy emphasis on Dr; he also gives 2 Do's, and there is a relative lack of color in the Rorschach. Fragmentation is widely in evidence, as on Card I where on inquiry he seems to dissect the insect: ". . . head, thorax, abdomen, plus three pairs of things . . . also head with two things sticking out . . ."; on Card III he sees "people disjointed at the waist"; on Card IV the squirrel "looks disconnected," and on Card VI he sees the "beginning of a violin . . . not complete." The TAT stories are curious assemblies of little things rather than well-thought-out plots. A number of stories involve termination of relationships and feelings of remaining alone and isolated. On Card I the boy is being left alone and made to practice the violin that gets broken; on 6 BM the son is leaving the mother and she "will just have to accept this." In these and other stories the connections between ideas and feelings are often buried.

## 6. *Intellectualization,* Rating: 2.5

The subject makes prominent efforts to appear heavily invested in intellectual pursuits, but no really solid intellectual trends are seen in the tests. He has a verbal IQ of 126 and a total IQ of 125. His answers on the WAIS, however, are fairly simple (e.g., item 12 on Information subtest)—except for his more involved statements on the Comprehension subtest. He takes most of the questions at face value and produces little that is abstract or esoteric. On the TAT there is a mild emphasis on the older and wiser generation giving advice and explanations to the younger, but his stories are generally uncomplicated and often banal. On the Rorschach he had no more than 27 responses; his only W is a simple one; he had only 1½ M, and there is no wide range in content. All in all, his Rorschach performance, except for the "lung experiment" on Card X, shows no noteworthy intellectual drive.

## 7. *Rationalization,* Rating: 3

This category receives a slightly higher rating than intellectualization since emphasis is somewhat greater on common-sense justification of statements than on abstract and intellectual ones.

## 8. *Undoing,* Rating: 1

None is present or observable in this record.

## 9. *Introjection and identification*

a. *With aggressor,* Rating: 3.5.   In the Rorschach, aggressive content is evident on Card III ". . . a very young sprout of a plant of some sort. Top—roots were broken off after being pulled out." On Card VII there is a "stump" instead of the usual "tail" on the popular animals, and on Card X the subject's first response is "a ripped appearance—like a piece of lettuce"; and we may refer again to the "lung experiment." The TAT contains a number of stories which represent aggressive interaction: the punishment of the boy who shoots and kills a kidnaper (8 BM); the hypnotist who will be helpful only until a new ailment arises (12 M); the child born out of wedlock (Picasso). A variety of other themes point to identification with the aggressor (1, 3 BM, 6 BM). It should be noted that an orientation towards aggressive interaction seems to be a relatively enduring part of the make-up of this subject, at least on the level of fantasy, and it therefore goes beyond the simple affect rating.

b. *Altruistic,* Rating: 1.5.   Altruistic trends are not evident in the test record. There is a lack of understanding of the child labor item on the WAIS, and the subject seems incapable of dealing with the problem in the way it is posed. Similarly he dissociates himself from "bad company," as if motivated by a fear that ordinary social mores may be lost quite easily. On Card 6 BM of the TAT he mentions that the hero's mother might feel lonely, but it is stated dryly and without much empathy. The remark seems to reflect aloofness and self-centeredness. No questioning, no elaborating the responsibility or concern the hero might feel in regard to the situation; a flat statement: the mother must simply accept this. The only story in the whole record with any altruistic connotation, and that a mild one, is given to Card 10 where a widow receives support from her brother after her husband's death.

### 10. *Over-all defensive success*, Rating: 2.5

This rating falls between "moderately successful" and "spotty" defensive efforts. It seems likely that the projective trends evidenced in the record serve to reinforce the subject's more general isolation defense. His ego is obviously not in full, adequate, and flexible control; it is sufficiently dominated by offensive-aggressive feelings, by guilt, and by frustration and depression. His use of projection also seems at times to lead to somewhat peculiar responses.

### D. Superego

### 1. *Severity*, Rating: 3.5

On the TAT a number of themes seem to express guilt feelings. The kidnaping on Card 8 BM refers to a feeling of guilt which seems almost irrational, and guilt is likewise expressed over the friend who is found dead (3 BM) and the broken violin (1). There is a rigidity about moral issues: the prostitute (13 MF), the child born out of wedlock (Picasso); and some empty emphasis on good and bad in the Comprehension subtest. The subject's depressive orientation seems to include an almost constant preoccupation with anger which cannot find expression; this might point toward trends of guilt.

### 2. *Integration*, Rating: 1.5

This subject's behavior is likely to be quite consistent with standards. As previously pointed out, he gives only a few indications of impulsivity or lability. In fantasy he does seem to have aggressive thoughts and rather violent ideas, but he does not appear to be a person who acts them out.

## E. Adaptive Strengths

### 1. *Adequacy of reality testing,* Rating: 3

The WAIS responses are quite adequate in terms of this category. There are no bizarre statements and only one or two moderately distorted responses. His definition of "matchless" on Vocabulary and his response to "Why should people pay taxes" may be considered somewhat deviant. On the Rorschach his F + per cent is 79–84; there are no confabulations or contaminations, and he has seven populars. Thus there is no evidence for major lapses; however, occasional lapses do occur, as in the case of the "sprout" and the "reptilian feet" on Card III, the "typewriter" on Card VI, and the "ripped lettuce" on Card X. No gross perceptual distortions are to be found in any of the TAT pictures, although idiosyncratic elaborations occur on Cards 3 BM and 8 BM. On Card 13 MF the man whom the subject describes as the father is usually perceived as being young, a boy-friend, or fiance.

### 2. *Degree of synthesis within the ego,* Rating: 2

In the discussion above of the category of "Prominent Affects" a considerable gulf was pointed out between experienced and/or expressed emotions and feelings, and orientations he holds of which he is not consciously aware. This reflects weaknesses in ego integration. Lack of synthesis is evident also in specific Rorschach scores and content as represented by the single W, the high number of Dr's, and the fragmentation which has been discussed. All this indicates difficulty in generalizing and integrating the perceptual field, which may be expected to correspond to a noteworthy lack of ego synthesis on other levels also.

### 3. *Stress tolerance,* Rating: 3

We find some disruptions in the test records, but, as previously stated, no major lapses. In general the subject handles stressful situations in the tests reasonably well, he conforms quite well to the demands of the WAIS, and there are no major break-

downs of functions on the Rorschach. He recovers fairly readily
from temporary regressions as indicated by the relative lack of
persistence of idiosyncratic responses.

*4. Amount of committable energy available for adaptive tasks,*
Rating: 2

In the testing situation there is a lack of real involvement
with the exception of two of the WAIS performance subtests,
where the subject manifested considerable interest. His work
effort and enthusiasm seem somewhat restricted. He goes through
the TAT with a certain amount of pain and doubt and gives the
impression of trying very hard to complete it rapidly. There is
considerable absorption in aggressive fantasies and depressive
feelings, so that he has relatively less psychic energy freely available for adaptive tasks.

*5. Strength and variety of experienced affects*

a. *Strength,* Rating: 2.5.   It is clear that in this subject's case
affect strength should be rated higher than affect variety. His
affective responsivity is actually quite limited, as reflected in the
sum C of the Rorschach, the rather narrow experience balance,
the high Dr per cent, and the bland and rather brief TAT stories.
An affective "tone" is not altogether absent, but it is quite
constrained and seems to revolve primarily around aggression
and hostility.

b. *Variety and complexity,* Rating: 2.   The test record gives
little evidence of a greater variety and modulation of feelings and
affects. Their range seems quite restricted. The one manifestation
of acknowledged feeling is in his story on Card 16, the only
cheerful statement in the whole record.

*6. Profundity and variety of thought contents*

a. *Profundity,* Rating: 2.5   The subject's relative lack of intellectualization has been previously discussed. His WAIS is on the
whole fairly banal, only on the Comprehension subtest does he go
beyond the obvious. He seems to have some difficulty in express-

ing himself clearly and precisely. For instance, he pointed out a number of times in the WAIS that his response was "a poor way to say it." None of the TAT pictures brought forth any intellectually exciting or particularly abstract stories. His Rorschach responses also lacked organization, elaboration, and intellectually significant content.

b. *Variety*, Rating: 2.    In the case of the present subject this rating corresponds fairly clearly to "profundity." The emptiness previously mentioned is found here too. He indicates some interest in chemistry but there is no broader representation of concern with a wider area of thought content. The very banality of his responses seems to exclude the possibility of considerable variety in his thinking generally.

## 7. *Regression in the service of the ego*

a. *Over-all rating*, Rating: 2. The subject's rather marked reluctance to allow himself to experience or express his own irrational trends is indicated in the record by the relative lack of M as well as the low Sum C. Variety and intensity of his fantasy are thus as limited as his spontaneity of emotional expression. Qualitatively, a rather pronounced trend in the record implies an attempt fairly strictly to adhere to realism and rationality. This is evident, for instance, in his response to Card 15 on the TAT: the subject decided that he could make something like an Edgar Allan Poe story here, but then states that, "being more realistic," he would settle for a much more commonplace story. His story to the Line Drawing also is introduced with the comment: "I wouldn't say that this is a realistic picture." Similarly, his failure, on first presentation, of Rorschach Card IX seems to manifest quite a strong and rapid blocking of possibilities for further regression. In instances where he does produce highly personal responses with regressive aspects, he does so with little pleaure and also rather little elaboration. This seems true, for instance, of the whole sequence of responses to Card III of the Rorschach. His attitude toward his own test productions is somewhat doubtful and exemplifies quite well the "unwilling, hesitant, and surprised concern with irrationality" which is the definition for step 2 of this scale.

b. *Creative output,* Rating: 2. Although the subject does give some unusual and highly personal responses, they possess little originality in the sense of a creation that appeals to others. Also relevant here seems to be the rather limited amount of total response output and particularly the rather limited integration and elaboration of his responses. He produces only one W in his record, and on the whole his TAT stories outline the plot but do not work it out in detail. The over-all emphasis of his responses is more on realism and correctness than on creation.

c. *Wit, humor, and playfulness,* Rating: 1.5. There are many opportunities in the testing situation to produce wit and humor. It can be done on the Comprehension subtest of the WAIS or in the Rorschach, particularly in the inquiry, or in the TAT. The subject makes no use of such opportunities. In only one instance does he show some enjoyment: on the blank card (16) of the TAT. There, for the moment, is a playful and joyous childhood scene. However, even there his direct expression of pleasure is moderated by the exactness of his definition of the location and depth of the snow, and by the quick end put to the children's fun by parental figures. In other instances, too, such as the "pastry" response on the Rorschach, he avoids possible humorous elaborations; rather in the inquiry he chooses to describe details of the "shadow" of the pastry. It sounds more like a problem of geometrical or technical drafting than any possible playfulness in interpretation. His few human responses in the Rorschach are serious and somewhat puzzled. On Card VII of the Rorschach, which is often used for the expression of playful themes, he does mention a puppy and in the inquiry says it is young; still he remains more concerned with defining the percept exactly than with elaborating on it. Thus a very low rating on this scale seems in order.

## 8. Social adaptiveness

a. *Ability to change oneself,* Rating: 2.5. Experience has shown that this rating is easier to make on the basis of interview data than of test information. Evidence from which to make a judgment is often fairly indirect. For example, the fact that the tests suggest no extreme rigidity but betray some instances of it is applicable here. That he may possess only a moderate variety of interpersonal responses is suggested by the subject's TAT stories. The relative containedness of his color responses also implies limited fluidity of his emotional functioning; and his apperception mode, rather heavily weighted on the side of rare details, H details and the like, would also seem to reflect a stubborn clinging to the details of a situation rather than a more fluid or flexible approach. Furthermore, certain signs of moralism and rationalism, which tell the subject how things ought to be, imply a sense of stable objective standards and thus, indirectly, a relative lack of autoplastic flexibility. On the other hand, he seems sufficiently doubtful of himself and open to advice (see TAT, 7). Thus it would appear that under proper environmental pressure he may be inclined to change himself, and his rigidity is certainly not so great that it altogether precludes minor autoplastic changes.

b. *Ability to change or influence others,* Rating: 2. Again, having only test results available, we would look for indirect evidence of such factors perhaps as empathic potential and extroverted concern for other people, as well at least as some amount of self-certainty about issues the subject thinks important. With regard to empathy the relative lack of M responses seems noteworthy, as well as the relative lack of statements that might indicate interpersonal sensitivity. But, perhaps most important, the over-all quality of his test record is one of somewhat anxious stagnation than of active striving or domineering driving motives. Thus it is not clear in what direction the subject would influence other people if he had the potential for it. A minimal rating of 1, on the other hand, does not seem appropriate either. Such a rating would probably be appropriate for instances of more pervasive passivity than this record provides.

c. *Flexibility of social exploration and affiliation,* Rating: 2x. Considerations of rigidity would again apply here; and nowhere in this subject's test responses do we find references to the processes of becoming acquainted with others, to active social interests, or to concerns with social groups. Nowhere does a strong affiliation motive appear. To the degree that his TAT responses, especially, suggest some concern with interpersonal encounters, one finds him expressing attitudes of dependency, assertion, or affection mostly in relation to a single other person.

His social explorativeness thus seems limited, but the evidence is unclear so only a doubtful rating can be made.

d. *State of social adaptation*, Rating: 2. Relevant here among other things would seem to be a scrutiny of the subject's H responses. On Card I of the Rorschach there is the figure of the woman but it is indistinct, unclear, and vague. The popular humans on Card III are seen with something of an aura of estrangement; he sees them as "dark shapes, disjointed" and with "reptilian feet." The same is true of his responses to the TAT; his story to card 10 where a man comforts his brother's widow does contain some positive affect, but of a rather superficial sort and slightly inappropriate, since the brother says, "All will turn out for the best." The actual implication seems to be an unconscious exploitation of the situation by the brother, which again does not imply the motive of pleasurable social affiliation. On the whole, the number of human responses in the Rorschach is limited. Furthermore, the subject tends to underplay the human element in his responses; on the Comprehension subtest on the WAIS he is more concerned with the application of rules and principles.

9. *Drive regulation, utilization, and implementation,* Rating: 2.5–4.5

Of importance here is the relative discrepancy between, on the one hand, indications of rigidity and isolation of affects and drives, and on the other hand, certain temporary, regressive, idiosyncratic, and relatively undisguised expressions of drive issues. There is little evidence that the subject ever really "lets himself go"; efforts at self-control are clearly represented in his extended F per cent of 96 and extended F+ per cent of 84, and there are many indications, previously discussed, of his holding tightly to reality. And yet we find fairly direct manifestations of drive impulses which are poorly integrated into the rest of his functioning and show aspects of lability. The responses of "pillows" and "sherbet" on Card VIII of the Rorschach as well as the "pastry" on Card V seem to be expressions of orally receptive impulses. They appear with relative suddenness in the record and are fairly isolated from his other responses. Thus, this subject shows some temporary regressions with aspects of being momentarily outside the service of the ego. He seems generally to vacillate between somewhat rigid control of drives and temporary lapses of drive regulation. Relevant also are the apparent moralistic inhibitions of sexuality which appear in the stories to the Picasso picture and to Card 13 MF of the TAT. The inconsistencies described seem best expressed in a split rating.

### F. Sense of Self

1. *Control vs. being influenced,* Rating: 3.5.

A scrutiny of the TAT stories suggests a general balance on the side of being influenced. More things seem to happen to people than are done by them. In the first story the violin is broken and the hero is exposed to punishment, a dead friend is found in the next story, and on Card 4 somebody seizes the opportunity to get away from a situation in which he is being influenced, a scene repeated in a similar manner on Card 6 BM. Although in the latter two stories some assertive steps are taken, these seem to result more from the pressure of circumstances than from constructive, actively executed motives. In general it appears that the subject senses quite strongly manifestations of activity and assertiveness, even though such strivings are present in a latent, defended-against way. His behavior in the testing situation also implies a passive submission to requirements. He often looked for further instructions, as when he asked: "Is it all right to hold it upside down?"—referring to a Rorschach card. The previous comment about his relative lack of strong active motives would also be applicable here.

2. *Involvement (active or passive) vs. detachment,* Rating: 4

The conception of self underlying these rating scales is derived in part from Gestalt psychological connotations; thus the rating on F 1 is expected to express something like a balance of strength between the Gestalt of the self and its surroundings. The ratings on the second variable reflect something like the sharpness of contour of the self or the permeability of its boundary. In this subject's record, detachment seems to predominate, as suggested by the high F+ and F% in his Rorschach, the emphasis on fairly clearly bounded percepts, particularly in his dr's, and his sense of distance from other people. There are some exceptions, momentary instances of concreteness on the Rorschach—the more regressive oral responses of sherbet and lettuce, in particular, imply fleeting occasions of involvement. But on the whole there seems to be little excitement about issues of any kind, intellectual or interpersonal. One minor response expresses quite well his general detachment from his surroundings, though it also contains a nostalgic element. On the Picture Completion Test of the WAIS, item number 18, he says, "I can't see anything specific missing other than the tree looks alone."

### 3. *Expansion of relationships with the not-self vs. constriction,* Rating: 3.5

Referring again to Gestalt notions of the self, it is hoped to indicate on this scale something about the direction in which the self changes in relation to its environment, about its enhancement, or its shrinkage. The subject's response to all tests implies an attitude of unsureness and doubtfulness, and a sense of distance. His reponse has a certain pessimistic quality; he seems more to stagnate rigidly and moralistically than to be a joyful explorer in the world. This person is far from thinking the world is his oyster.

### 4. *Homogeneity of the self vs. conflict,* Rating: 3.5

Again in this rating emphasis must be given to the relatively more conscious aspects of the sense of self. The subject seems to think of himself as less conflicted than the test results suggest he really may be. On the other hand, there are indications that he lacks internal homogeneity. The people on Card III of the Rorschach with "reptilian feet," the percepts of the "uprooted tree," "ripped seaweed," "ragged, sloppy bow tie" all point in the direction of a sense of conflict. They would refer particularly to some components of the self—to the body image and self-evaluations. As we have already mentioned, certain responses suggest a somewhat depressive trend. Yet it should be noted that the subject's TAT stories, for instance, usually place manifestations of conflict in the relationships between people. There are, further, fairly rigid defenses, and although manifestations of anxiety are present they are not overwhelming.

### 5. *Body image*, Rating: 4

Some inferences from the preceding paragraph apply here. We might again consider the "disjointed people" on the Rorschach, the "ragged bow tie," the "torn seaweed," the "stump of a tail." There is furthermore, on Card X, the strange "experiment on the lungs." These responses do not imply a positive view of the body as an intact and smoothly functioning asset. On the TAT other references may be relevant: on Card 1 the broken violin, on Card 3 the dead friend, on Card 7 the dirty prostitute.

### 6. *Acceptance of the self vs. rejection*, Rating: 3.5

What has been said about this subject's depressive components, his guilt, his strict moralism, his sense of distance from others, his general level of frustration, seems applicable here as well. But his defensiveness may help him to keep altogether from consciousness insights which are too unpleasant.

### G. Psychosocial Modalities

#### A. *Subject's standing on each modality*

1. *Trust vs. basic mistrust*, Rating: 3.5.   On the more social level, relevant test data in this case might be the following: on Card 13 of the TAT the subject implies that somebody cannot trust his daughter, on the Picasso drawing he emphasizes the child born out of wedlock and describes some of the complications, on the "iron" item of the Comprehension subtest he speaks of the "victim of the striking" who may have been unprepared. Less outstanding instances might be the implication on Card 6 BM of the TAT that the mother-figure must inevitably be disappointed, and on Card 12 M that a cure will not be permanent. On more regressive levels, it seems relevant that the "pastry" on the fifth Rorschach card is not really a pastry but the shadow of one, as though the subject were saying one cannot trust the reality of objects. The content of the pastry response is oral, as is

the "sherbet" response on Card VIII of the Rorschach and the "lettuce" response on Card X. The percept of the "uprooted tree" on Card III seems to imply a projection of the sense of being separated from one's nourishing ground. There seems the further likelihood that the "pillows" on Card VIII of the Rorschach, with the elaboration of their being "roundish and plump," yet also "wrinkled," with "indentations," may be representations of breasts, which have shriveled. Finally, we might look at some of the formal aspects of trust and mistrust. In extremely suspicious, distrustful people we would for instance expect rather elevated subtest scores on the Picture Arrangement and Picture Completion subtests of the WAIS, but in this instance neither are particularly high.

2. *Autonomy vs. shame and doubt,* Rating: 4.  There is some emphasis on the issue of autonomy, but strivings for assertion and independence are usually seen by this subject in the context of frustration. On card 1 of the TAT the assertive act of breaking the violin leads to punishment; on Card 4 the man strives for independent action, but it is somewhat aimless and seems more in response to control exerted by the woman. On the other hand, there are quite a few expressions, direct and indirect, of the sense of shame or doubt. On card 8 BM of the TAT we find the painful exposure of the daughter; and in the subject's manner of handling items on the WAIS there seems to be a fair amount of shame, as when he protectively says he does not know an item and then guesses it wrong. He has doubts about his own ability and seems to depend on authority, although he is doubtful of authority: in the "forest" item of the Comprehension test he emphasizes that moss will not always serve as a good authority to indicate direction. The "tree" in the Picture Completion test stands somewhat conspicuously in isolation. The subject's failure on Card IX of the Rorschach in relation to defensiveness also seems to indicate a rather low degree of assertiveness. A definition of the scale step 4 indicates possible rebelliousness against one's own insignificant status, and this definition (although basically it must remain doubtful) seems appropriate to the subject's performance.

3. *Initiative vs. guilt,* Rating: 3.5. On the level most close to drive expression we would look here for percepts of a phallic kind. They are not entirely absent from the record. On Card VII of the Rorschach the subject sees a "puppy with the tail stuck

out and the ears up," but it is a puppy and not a grown dog; on Card VII the usual animals have a "stump of a tail." On the "iron" item in the Comprehension test the emphasis is on the victim being struck, rather than on the person who does the striking. On the more social levels are several expressions of guilt over initiative. These can be found on Card 6 BM of the TAT; on Cards 4 and 7 BM the man's striving for independence is at the same time a show of rather poor judgment. In general, where there are manifestations of aggression they seem of a more inhibited kind than might be put to use constructively, in goal-directed  strivings. On the whole guilt seems somewhat to predominate, but there is no evidence, on the other hand, for a marked paralysis of initiative.

4. *Industry vs. inferiority*, Rating: 3.5.    Evidence relevant to a rating on the entire issue is fairly scant in the tests. However it may be said that in the subject's TAT stories in particular little emphasis is placed on production or the making of things; there is much more focus on interpersonal orientations and attitudes and their difficulties. A sense of future goals or of productivity finds scant expression; in the context of his test responses, the concepts of accomplishment and achievement are lacking. His test performance itself is not an industrious one; it suggests, in fact, a sense of inferiority—in the relatively low number of responses on the Rorschach, the failure on Card IX, the general uncertainty of his Wechsler responses.

5. *Identity vs. identity diffusion*, Rating: 3.5.    Two aspects of the test performance are relevant: one, the degree of integration within the person, the other the degree of integration with the person's surroundings, particularly with other people. Considering the TAT especially, on the more social level there are indications of much strife and contradiction between hero figures and others: others inhibit, they give advice, they punish or suppress, but little integration with them seems possible. Here are indications, also, of a general lack of direction, mentioned previously: no clearly focused achievement motive, sexual motive, or assertive motive. Within the subject himself there seems to be a relative lack of inner homogeneity. We have spoken of the evidence relating to body image and sense of conflict; it applies here, too. In addition one might consider the quality of his Rorschach H responses; there are only two, and his approach to

these implies a lack of that solid confrontation of others we would expect to find in a person with a strongly developed sense of personal identity. On the other hand, there are no signs of utter fragmentation or diffusion. Nor is there evidence of marked inconsistent going against others or a fundamental conflict dividing the self into warring parties. Therefore, a more extreme rating on identity diffusion seems inappropriate.

6. *Intimacy vs. isolation*, Rating: 4. Much of the evidence previously quoted applies here again. The subject is somewhat distant from others, he does not confront them directly with ease; his capacity is meager for self abandonment and yielding himself while retaining the ability to recover himself with certainty. In general it may be said that the more complex variables defined in the later part of the rating system increasingly tend to imply information contained in earlier, more molecular categories.

7. *Generativity vs. stagnation*, Rating: X. The definition of generativity and the theoretical formation of this concept in Erikson's writing show it to be a rather mature achievement. Our subject is relatively young; his lack of generativity in the sense of the definition should not therefore be considered indicative of stagnation. Rather it is more appropriate to consider this dimension not yet applicable to a person his age. Therefore the X rating. It would be equally inappropriate to rate ten-year-olds on the category of identity. In them, to be sure, are precursors and early consolidations of identity, just as there are groping attempts at generativity in a nineteen-year-old. But these are only precursors, and the categories defined here refer to the psychosocial issues as they chronologically and genetically move into full focus.

## B. *Degree of emphasis of each modality*

1. *Trust vs. basic mistrust*, Rating: 3.5. Relevant to this rating are the emphases on orality detailed above, lack of pleasantness and warmth in interpersonal relations, absence of optimism, pessimism, and the previously outlined minor depressive trend. A higher rating than this would be appropriate if there were more pronounced and obvious trust or more tangible mistrust; for instance, manifestations of more strongly developed paranoid attitudes or more severe depressive components.

2. *Autonomy vs. shame and doubt*, Rating: 3. The qualita-

tive aspects of manifestation of this issue have been discussed before. Quantitatively speaking, autonomy versus shame and doubt is somewhat less emphasized than the trust issue, although clearly still an issue laden with conflict. Therefore the above rating seems appropriate.

3. *Initiative vs. guilt*, Rating: 3.5. Prominent evidence related to this issue is the subject's inhibition of a sense of striving and assertion. This inhibition seems to extend to the sexual, interpersonal, or similarly oriented areas. On the whole we find a fair amount of struggle and unsettledness here.

4. *Industry vs. inferiority*, Rating: 2.5. This issue is less prominently represented in the subject's test record, where achievement striving and task orientation appear relatively little. Yet a noteworthy sense of inferiority shows up, which seems closely related to the subject's doubt, shame, and guilt.

5. *Identity vs. identity diffusion*, Rating: 4. This issue is importantly represented. The qualitative evidence was quoted above; quantitatively there are many references of this kind in the Rorschach and in the TAT. The issue is prominent and central at the present time.

6. *Intimacy vs. isolation*, Rating: 3.5. Throughout the test record, the subject's relationships with other people and his difficulty with those relationships are fairly obvious.

7. *Generativity vs. stagnation*, Rating: X. Reasons for making no judgment on this variable were described under the corresponding heading in part A (page 119).

In general, this case is outstanding because of a relative lack of extreme ratings on all variables. In the test records or interview material of most subjects we find a great deal more variation and much sharper distinctions between the emphases given different issues or character traits. This subject somewhat lacks color. Experience has shown that cases such as his are harder to rate on assessment categories than subjects with great intrapersonal variation.

## H. Character Elaborations

These ratings are those of the greatest complexity in the entire assessment scheme. They come closest to a clinical summary of the subject, though they do not affix a label but rather provide a profile of each subject on a number of categories. The evidence on which these ratings are to be based is that underlying all previous ratings. Judgments on the dimensions of character elaborations in a way tend to summarize previous judgments; for each characterological rating in this category there are certain relevant ratings in the categories of affect, defenses, adaptive strengths, psychosocial modalities, and cognitive styles. Thus, in discussing our subject's standing in these various categories, we will often not refer back to the original test evidence but simply summarize previous ratings.

## 1. *Narcissistic*, Rating: 2

For a high rating on this variable, we would expect a person to show a greater amount of aloofness and egocentricity and less responsiveness to other people than our subject does. In his test records there is evidence of conflict and uncertainty in relation to other people, but no convincing sign that toward other people there is actually a lack of cathexis. Some narcissistic trends can be seen in his infantile, oral, ungiving, self-centered orientation. In his suspiciousness, too, we may find traces of narcissism. A rating of 2 suggests the presence of noteworthy instances of the variable in question, but it also indicates that this is not really a predominant orientation. It might further be said that the narcissistic position is not dependent on any very specific defense; narcissistic orientation on the whole is a defensive attitude against object involvement in general.

## 2. *Hysterical*, Rating: 2.5

Signs of a hysterical orientation are relatively weak; there is no great amount of emotional lability, or of phobic or anxious trends. On the other hand, there are indications of repression and infantility. The important hysterical attribute of a naïve moralism usually connected with repressive defenses is also only minimally present, although some of the TAT stories, such as to Card 8 BM and to the Picasso, or his response to the child labor law item, do suggest moralistic trends. Again no striking instances of hysterical attributes appear, so a rating of 2.5 would be appropriate.

## 3. *Obsessive*, Rating: 3.5

There is some evidence of intellectualization as a permanent ego defense, and of noteworthy attempts at perfectionism. The subject is trying to be unsentimental and objective; for instance, in his response to Card X of the Rorschach where he sees the experiment on the lungs.

## 4. *Feminine-masculine*, Rating: 1.5

Important test evidence here would involve not only direct evidence of femininity but some emphasis on passivity, tenderness, and nurturance. There is no noteworthy evidence of the sort. The subject seems neither feminine nor effeminate and, although infantile and in part orally oriented, shows no signs of specific sexual inversion.

## 5. *Dependent*, Rating: 3

Evidence of his need for dependable authorities can be found in some of the subject's relatively simple-minded notions of morality and in the ambivalence of all descriptions of attempts to gain independence in his TAT stories. Despite the signs of dependency we have mentioned, particularly a marked evidence of oral preoccupation, he does not appear to be a happily dependent person in whom dependent traits are fully ego-syntonic. There is a good deal of conflictful striving for self-assertion in his resentment of control (as in his TAT story to card 4) so that dependency does not reach the rating of 4 which would indicate a predominantly dependent orientation.

## 6. *Sado-masochistic*, Rating: 3.5

Of this variable there is some fairly pronounced evidence. We saw it in the "iron" item in the Comprehension test and in various TAT stories where fighting is either implied or directly mentioned. Aggression is much more indirectly expressed, in both its destructive and harmed implications, in his emphasis on ripping, raggedness and the like in several Rorschach responses. It seems clear that sado-masochistic evidence is stronger than the evidence of dependency mentioned above and justifies a rating of 3.5.

## 7. *Passive-aggressive*, Rating: 2.5

While there is no overt, unambivalent expression of aggression, there are nevertheless hints that aggression is recognized as such and inhibited, but that it essentially strives for fairly direct discharge. Evidence of behind-the-back and very indirect aggression is lacking. In Card 1 of the TAT, for instance, the breaking of the violin is an indirectly aggressive manifestation, but in most of the other stories involving aggression it takes a much more direct course. Nevertheless, passive aggressive trends are not altogether absent and therefore a rating close to the midpoint seems appropriate.

## 8. *Hypomanic*, Rating: 1

Evidence of a tendency to be overly optimistic, hyperactive, enterprising and helpful is clearly missing. There is very little euphoria. Affects appearing in the test record tend on the whole more to the disphoric side, and the relevant defense mechanism of denial is not strongly represented.

## 9. *Schizoid*, Rating: 2

This category must be clearly differentiated from the narcissistic. Schizoidness would be rated by marked evidences of fantasy possessing magical, mystical, peculiar, idealistic, or abstruse qualities. Although the schizoid person as defined here holds himself aloof from other people, as would the narcissistic person, schizoid withdrawal from life is greater and reality contact much less well maintained. In this particular case instances of blandness on the one hand, or extraordinary sensitivity on the other, are lacking. As mentioned above, evidence of fantasy is minimal; however, the subject does show a tendency toward withdrawal and keeping his distance from other people, and some of his responses have a rather peculiar quality. This is especially true of certain Rorschach responses we discussed earlier. Therefore, a rating seems appropriate which takes these noteworthy instances into consideration.

### 10. *Projective,* Rating: 2

Again, there is no overriding evidence, although indications are present. In his WAIS, for example, the subject's relatively low Picture Completion test score would imply a lack of projective hyperalertness. If there is some suspiciousness, it is more in the sense of pessimism than of searching out the motives of other people, finding hidden meanings or the like. On the other hand, projective trends are not altogether absent, as indicated by the idiosyncratic quality of certain Rorschach responses, and the somewhat peculiar story about the hypnotist on the TAT, in which the implication is that things are going on which one cannot understand.

### 11. *Psychopathic,* Rating: 1

Lability and acting out are conspicuous by their absence, as indicated by the subject's rather minimal color series in the Rorschach, and, further, his moralistic notions and fairly marked guilt feelings. There are no indications of trends of manipulation.

### 12. *Diffusion,* Rating: 2.5

In this record there is some evidence of diffusion. We have previously discussed some of the subject's identity problems, his internal conflict and his lack of a sense of where he is going. We find, besides, ambivalence in his interpersonal relationships and his sense of self, and, as described above, a mixture of dependency and anger in his relations to others, in his case best understood, in part at least, as a transitory developmental phenomenon. Here, as in the relative rigidity of some of his defenses (his moralism and the like), there are many indications of possible stability; by no means should this subject be understood to be diffused in the sense in which a tramp or a shiftless character from the Bowery is diffused.

### 13. As-if, Rating: 1

It is very difficult to say if someone is more or less an as-if character. Therefore, only ratings of 1 or 4 or 5 are permissible. In this case there is very little evidence of the lack of internal structuredness characteristic of an as-if person. Indications that the subject comes into conflict with others from time to time are enough to contradict the "chameleon-like adaptiveness" specified by the definition of this scale.

### 14. Counterphobic, Rating: 1

The presence of some anxiety, internal conflict, and masochistic elements in the sado-masochistic orientation speaks against the presence of counterphobic trends. Nowhere in the record is there any indication of superior assertion or of attack as a means of defense against anxiety or threat. Even in the TAT story involving kidnaping, the person who defends himself and kills one of the kidnapers feels guilty. Evidence on this variable is therefore minimal.

### 15. Depressive, Rating: 3.5

Relevant here are evidences of the subject's preponderant oral orientation and his relative lack of a sense of closeness to people, of adequacy, self-assurance, and the like. It appears that he is not dominated by severe depressive moods or affects which paralyze him; but there are signs of a fairly continuous, slightly agitated, chronic depressive orientation. His primitive functions, his demandingness expressed in some of the oral responses, his sense of distance from others and some feelings of doubt about his assertiveness all serve as evidence. There are thus striking instances of the presence of depressive trends.

### 16. Genital, Rating: 1.5

Erikson once said that each system must have its utopia; that of the genital character is the psychoanalytic utopia. According to the scale definitions, there is very little evidence that this subject fulfills the criteria for a higher rating on this scale. His relationships to others are ambivalent. He is selective in his response to external stimuli. His capacity to love and establish a full emotional relationship to others is limited, and partial drives, particularly the oral and sado-masochistic, have not yet found their way into a more integrated unity. A low rating is appropriate.

Although the discussion of subject A's ratings on the different scales focused on varying aspects of his character structure it is also clear that we encountered recurrent manifestations of similar trends and themes which would seem to characterize subject A especially, constituting an essential expression of his individuality. Their identification and formulation may yield something approaching a statement of the overdetermined or Gestalt aspects of subject A's character structure. Or perhaps it could be said that these recurrent trends or themes represent a set of variables of greater generality than the dimensions in the scheme. If we assume the latter, we would, theoretically, have to keep in mind the possibilities that such more general variables represent something like interindividually, reasonably stable factors, such as might also be determined by a statistical factor analysis of the assessment scheme, or else that these more general variables are a matter of quite individual structure formations and of patterns of functions. In the following paragraphs we shall not attempt to reach a decision on this question but we will rather try to describe some of subject A's characteristically recurrent trends and themes. We can approach this attempt by scrutinizing especially those instances where subject A received relatively high or low ratings on the scales; they are more likely to highlight individual trends than do the ratings closer to the mid-points of the scales.

The first conspicuous fact in subject A's case is the relative absence of really extreme ratings. There are no ratings of 5, and low ratings of 1 appear almost exclusively in the group of "Character Elaborations" where they connote more the absence or the relative inapplicability of the trend represented by the scale than a positive and characteristic expression of an individual position.

From all this we may perhaps infer a relative inconspicuousness of the subject's character structure in general. Summarizing information from the subject's ratings on scales in quite different groups and, for the sake of brevity, not referring to these scales in detail and by number, we find that the configuration of his ratings would tend to support our assumption of a trend of inconspicuousness. We find subject A as rather detached, somewhat mistrustful, and quite dominated by doubt and shame. He is described by the ratings as being very much in a position of isolation and of lack of intimacy. His social adaptability lacks flexibility and intensity and the ratings describe him as rather lacking in spontaneity.

There is a concomitant theme of some internal limitations of the richness of thought content or of emotional experience. His capacity to regress within himself and in a controlled and introspective manner is described as rather low, particularly also in the areas of "wit, humor, and playfulness." Thus subject A seems not only detached, somewhat withdrawing, and unspontaneous in his relations to the environment and to others, but also within himself, particularly in terms of imagination and of emotion.

All this would seem to be related to, and partly to be an expression of, the effects of rather rigid defenses. We find subject A high on isolation and somewhat high on projection. Both of these defenses tend to heighten rigidity and emphasize somewhat sterile intellectual processes, and they are quite consistent with the described themes of detachment and lack of spontaneity. The relatively high rating on the "obsessive" character elaboration is another expression of the same trend.

A fourth major theme appears in the form of pressures of aggressive impulses. We find subject A described as identifying with the aggressor, as somewhat "sado-masochistic," but also as frequently feeling frustrated and thwarted. It would appear, as a subaspect of this theme, that some of this aggression is often turned upon the self: the subject is rated as experiencing strong guilt at times and as devaluating himself, especially in terms of his body, and there are indications of a depressive trend. All of these trends and themes appear to be controlled and integrated to only limited degrees; over-all ego-synthesis is only partially successful and the amount of internal conflict leads to a relative diminution of the amount of energy available for productive adaptation. The subject's identity on the whole is incompletely developed. At the same time the ratings in their total configuration also indicate no expressions of major or clinical pathology.

The foregoing comments do not pretend to be an exhaustive description of the interplay of dynamic factors within the subject's character structure. But they intend to serve as a tentative example of a summary, derived from the assessment ratings, of individually specific and significant characterological themes.


## SUBJECT B

Mr. G., Age 17, Freshman, Yale College, Single.
Father: Age 43, business executive.
Mother: Age 35, housewife.
Brothers: Ages 18 and 12.
Early environment: Quite transient, father was Navy officer until recently.
Religion: None (formerly Protestant).

The following protocol was gained from two interviews of one hour, 30 minutes each. Both were recorded with the subject's knowledge and were subsequently transcribed. The interviews covered certain predetermined contents, but they were not tightly structured. The material reproduced below is not a condensation, but represents some of the highlights of the three hours. This procedure was adopted, since it seemed important that the reader become familiar with both the content and the subject's style and quality of speech.


### Interview Protocol

I:1 We have two one-and-a-half hour sessions of interviews to try and find out more about you, your family and so forth. To start out would you take about fifteen minutes to tell me about yourself?

S:1   Okay. Well, I was born out in California in 1940. And then, I'm not sure exactly where we moved. See, my Dad was in the Navy at the time. We did a lot of moving during the war. I spent some time in San Diego and some in Washington, D.C., two years in South America, and then California for two years. That's when I was a freshman and sophomore in high school. And then to Honolulu for two more years, my junior and senior years of high school. I think Hawaii was the part that's had the most effect on me. And there in my junior year I didn't do anything but study just about, hit the books. And then my senior year was entirely different. I was elected to high office in school due to a—it was purely luck. I didn't know hardly anyone having just come there my junior year, but I made a good speech. So I had that, and then I joined the ROTC and became an officer my senior year, so that was a good experience. And then I was in the science club. And in the Sabre and Chain Club. I made Honor Society and things like that. In other words my senior year was really I think the time when I first came out to life, sort of. I was sort of an introvert more or less up until that time. Not really an introvert, I wasn't sort of outgoing, but that was the time I really got to know people more or less and did a little bit in life. Between my brother and I, who is a year older, but in the same grade, we had our finger in a lot of pies out there. So we were in a ruling status, which is pleasant. When I first came to Yale I hated it very much because it was a— first of all, there were no girls around. I was used to dating girls quite often and having them all around me. I got a scholarship to Yale so I decided to come here. I wasn't sure I'd made the right choice. But then since then I've changed my mind. I wouldn't trade Yale for the world because I'm thinking about getting out of engineering which is my major and going into I'm not sure what—just taking a liberal arts education, because I don't know what I want in life or what I want to be or what I want to do.

I:2   Could you take about five minutes and tell me what kind of person you are, how you think of yourself and how you feel about yourself?

S:2   Well, I think I'm not real intelligent as far as brains go. I feel that I get the grades that I do and feel that I've gotten into Yale because of not real hard work, but I don't feel I'm like a lot of people at Yale that just actually have the ability. In other words, I sort of feel I'm in a way in the wrong place as far as brains go, but I know I can always get decent grades because I do study and I do like to be at least in the top quarter of the class. And I can keep myself there if I work hard enough, but . . . (clears throat) I feel I'm very, very selfish in many respects. The way I—the reason I feel that more than anything else is through experience I've had with women. I feel that I'm —I demand too much as far as total devotion to myself goes on their part. I often ask myself if I ever did return the same for other people, and I get the conclusion I don't. And also because of my philosophy of life where I'm not trying to leave the world anything. I'm just trying to exist here for seventy years or thereabouts or whatever it turns out to be, and then leave. So I feel I'm basically selfish. But I feel I've got—feel that I feel things deeper than most people do. And I try to be a little different than most people. And I feel I understand people fairly well, understand others. And . . . like I said, I was—I'm an atheist so to speak. I'm an atheist, but then I don't—I'm not satisfied with my position as being an atheist. I'd like to be religious. And I'd like to have that security that religion gives. I was very religious. But then in my senior year, I got to questioning religion and things like that, very, very deeply and I came to the conclusion that I don't believe although I'd like to believe in God and religion. . . .

I:3   Tell me something about how having a father who was in the service has affected your life?

S:3   Well, of course, in the travel immediately it's given me a tremendous desire to travel. It's made me basically more restless than it would be if I'd been raised in a city, Arkansas, say, all my life, by traveling every two years. I'll never be able to—never be willing to settle down and stay in one place long. It's given me a broader outlook than I would have had otherwise, seeing the other side of things. Every two years just saying goodbye to every friend I ever had and starting all over again. And I'm always unhappy when it first happens, but you make new friends. And I think that the service has basically given me my philosophy of enjoying life. Because I think most service people—most men in the service enjoy life a whole lot and especially a lot of Navy captains seem to be the people, of all people I've ever seen on the whole enjoy life more than anyone else.

I:4  Was your father one of the people that enjoyed himself a great deal?

S:4  No, I don't think so really. I think my father is always been someone who's a perfectionist, absolute perfectionist and an extremely hard worker. I feel a certain way because I've seen the misery he goes through in demanding perfection so I know —I try not to demand perfection anymore. And I think he's . . . for example, when he got out of the Navy three months ago, he was going to come up for Admiral. But then he got this real good offer starting at much higher pay than he was making in the service. And so in other words he had the choice: to take what he enjoyed or take what he—to make money and to try to be a success so to speak and he's always wanted to be a success, I think, so he took that choice. And I think he made the wrong choice because he's not particularly happy in his job. So I don't think he's basically happy in life, and he is an atheist himself. . . .

I:5  The Navy was pretty important to him at the time?

S:5  Oh, I think so. Definitely. He's always been one of these Navy first and himself second type of person. Not by the book, I wouldn't say that.

I:6  Was he a disciplinarian?

S:6  Well, in a sense. We've always said "sir" to him. And when he gets mad, you . . . stand aside. He's always been— yeah, I'd say so—a disciplinarian, absolutely, but he's very tender, I think, inside. Maybe that's one reason why he is such a harsh disciplinarian, I think, because he is so warm inside.

I:7  How close were you and your brothers to your father?

S:7  We were close for a military family. My roommate here tells jokes to his Dad and slap each other on the back. We never had that kind of relationship. We've always known that he did love us and did care for us as children and that's what's important, whether he treats us strictly or disciplined I don't think really matters. When we were young we got strapped, my brother and I, when we did something wrong. And then we got the last strapping by him, my brother and I, that's when I was about twelve and my brother was thirteen. And my mother told me this later, that he vowed right then he'd never strap another kid again because it just hurt him so much to do it.

I:8   Would you get furious directly at him or—

S:8   Oh, no, not—I wouldn't dare do that—Well, I mean I'd show my anger and I'd . . . but I'd never act wise. There's no screaming or anything about it.

I:9   Is he kind of a frightening figure in some ways?

S:9   Not really, no. Because—if you understand him, see. I'd say that uh . . . he's not at all frightening. He's frightening when he gets mad—if he's angry, then definitely frightening. I wouldn't say it's a frightening figure really. I think he's very—like I say, basically very tender and very wonderful. Even my mother I think gets scared when he gets angry. He doesn't throw pictures at the wall or anything ridiculous like that. But he definitely gets more or less violent in his anger.

I:10   Are there certain things in your family that you're just not allowed to do?

S:10   I know swearing's one, I just don't swear around them. I mean, they know that I swear away from home.

I:11   Your father doesn't swear at home—

S:11   Oh, yes, he definitely swears. He swears quite frequently. I mean, he's . . . says—swears quite a bit. He never curses, but he swears, damn, hell, and things like that. He uses those words . . . quite often, I mean, it's quite natural. And uh . . . but we don't use it back to him, or we don't ever use it around the house. I don't think he'd really say anything in a way if we ever did. I think he'd just—it'd be more or less you'd feel he'd be disappointed in you if you did. Well, I don't—I don't know if he'd get—I know he wouldn't get violent or mad or anything like that if you did, but it'd just be a—you'd feel sort of silly doing it in a way—feel sort of silly swearing around him is the feeling I get . . . which isn't called for, so . . . I can't think of any other real taboos—I guess uh . . . with my mother her definite taboo is sex, real sex along with my father who didn't—wasn't really primarily interested in se—oh, you know, offend sex or an—for—he was quite a wild man when he was in college himself. At UCLA he had Phi Beta Kappa grades—all the way through, A's since his freshman year, straight A's, and at the same time he was a Kappa Beta Phi. It's reversed letters, it's a sort of a joke. If you're the big drinker at the fraternity and the big wild man you'd get a Kappa Beta Phi. Now my mother often mentioned if he had ever had a daughter, she pities the daughter. But as long as we're all men like himself, he's very, very liberal as far as sex matters, drinking and things like that—

I:12  Do you smoke in the house?

S:12  No, I don't smoke—none of my brothers or myself smoke but there again it's for uh—my father's a cancer nut. So there, it's for that reason that we don't smoke, not that they wouldn't allow us to, or anything like that—

I:13  He doesn't smoke.

S:13  Oh, yeah he smokes. Just one cigarette—one after breakfast and one after dinner. And my mother ss—used to smoke quite a bit, but then he got her to knock it off completely.

I:14  Did you get any sex education from him?

S:14  Oh, yeah. I can remember the birds and the bees stories first started down in Brazil and then uh—I guess that's probably what I was, yeah, twelve, thirteen. He educated us that way. He used to give us books, like *The Stork Didn't Bring You*. It's a—these books written nowadays, some are—and he used to have us read those . . . And that's the way he got us acquainted with sex—

I:15  Do you think he was uncomfortable talking to you about sex?

S:15  Well, up until high school I think he was. But then, for example, when I was going away to a military camp between my sophomore and junior year, ROTC, I was going to be going away for about a  month. So he just took me aside and told me frankly that if I did get mixed up with any girls and I did get venereal disease or anything like that, he said he'd kill me if I ever did it. But he said the first thing was come and tell him and he'd get me cured. And then he'd lose his wrath. So he was very practical about it. And—but I get the feeling that he was more or less uncomfortable talking about it—especially when you were young, I think it was—I think he was very uncomfortable anyway.

I:16  Did you feel free to ask him questions about sex?

S:16  No.

**I:17**  Could you ask your mother?

**S:17**  Yeah, well, she used to . . . well, you know, how mothers are about that—I never really discussed sex with my parents, but my mother would say things like uh I'd come home, I remember one time when I just shoved a girl in the pool. And I told my mother about it. I thought it was very funny that the girl said she couldn't go in. She was just being afraid of the cold water. And my mother took me aside and said, "Now listen, certain times girls can't go in the water. You understand that, don't you?" And so she filled me in on the story. So she uh she tells me when she feels it's essential I know, but we've never been really discussing sex with her—

**I:18**  Can you tell me something about the kind of group that your parents went around with, socially speaking—

**S:18**  Yeah. Well, in military, of course, it was obviously military friends. Of course, their—in military your social life is tremendous. And they've always—the very highest class people, absolutely. I've never seen my father—my father won't put up with a low class person, have him over or go to his house. He's very blunt about it. If he doesn't like somebody, he'll tell him so. And I mean it's people like four-star admirals, three-star admirals, generals, captains, his own rank, and uh he's uh and also a lot of contacts with uh important American officials. But people of the rank—of his own rank, colonel and captain of the navy and people in there, he—those were his—people he had over quite frequently. And they had—they'd have quite wild parties, you know, and get plastered and beat on bass drums and turn the old hi-fi set up real loud. They had a real great time. But they're all real good people.

**I:19**  What would you say was the aspect of military life that your father liked best?

**S:19**  Prestige was one thing. A lot of respect that other people afford you when you get up into a high rank. And uh— and he liked the social life . . . and the—and the general organization you'll find in the military—he's a very organized man. And see, the military to him wasn't so much of a job, eight hours a day, five days a week type thing. It was a continuous life.

**I:20**  How about politically?

**S:20** Oh, yeah, he's definitely a conservative. Doesn't like the liberal democratic idea. He'd probably prefer if uh if—he's never told me this—but he'd prefer enlightened aristocracy to rule.

**I:21** Could you tell me something about your mother?

**S:21** Well, she was uh born in Delaware, but was raised mostly in the Philippines. (Clears throat) And that's had a profound effect on her for this reason: out there she had a lot of servants and a lot of uh, you know, Americans are rel—are very wealthy relative to the Philippines. And she had a lot of, very easy life in that sense. She uh went to high school, never went to college, and married my father right after high school. I think she got married when she was seventeen. So she's got—due to this raising of, you know, wealthy family, and an aristocratic type family, relatively, out in the Philippines, she's definitely prejudiced, very prejudiced racially and very prejudiced uh on certain things to do. She's not education-wise, she's not very intelligent, but intellectually she's very brilliant. I can tell she's got a very bright mind.

**I:22** Can you describe her somewhat?

**S:22** Yeah, she's about—you mean physically? About five-five, I guess, brown hair, brown eyes . . . She's got a—when she was young she was very good looking.

**I:23** Mmhm . . . Well, you mentioned there—there was very little talk about sex with her, but for instance did you find out anything from her, or did she tell you anything about your toilet training or weaning?

**S:23** We never discussed things like that.

**I:24** How do you get along with your mother, and what kind of relationship do you have?

**S:24** Well, uh . . . well, I don't think I got along with my mother quite as well. In a sense I got along better, in a sense I didn't get along as well. In other words, my mother and I were— were uh closer simply because we were around each other more, you know, than my father. And we had a lot more time together and things like that. When I was going to school, she'd always be there when I came home, whereas my father wouldn't. He'd still be at work. And actually I guess it was uh . . . oh, I used always get—I-I-I had the feeling between—sometimes in my junior and senior year that she favored my older brother more than me. I think that's quite common, you know, for some people to have that. So I used to get furious at her for that. And that used to bo—I told her that once. And that bothered her no end. She got very hysterical. . . . But very unhappy when I told her that. Uh I had that feeling for quite awhile. But I . . . so I was never quite, you know, as much at ease with her for that reason, that I can remember. But before I got that (sniffs) feeling that she did, I think it was a very wonderful uh—just like with my father, a very standard relationship. And since I've ou—out-grown that feeling, it's very wonderful relationship again. I think we're very close and . . . and . . . I don't know—

**I:25** When you say that she became upset and hysterical, what do you mean?

**S:25** Well, she got . . . I mean, she was just sort of uh—she's a very emotional person. And she'd get uh uhm couldn't understand how I could feel that way and she—I think she cried once when I told her that. Was definitely very hurt by it. But uh . . . she was definitely a much much more less emotionally stable a person than my father. And I-I-I never had quite the respect for my mother that I had for my father for that—I guess it was the weakness of her fe-female sex or something, but I-I always thought her as a very n-nice person, a very wonderful person, but I didn't respect her in a sense that I respected my father as being the . . . characterwise I don't think she's as good as my father. I think she's more selfish than my father for one thing. And uh I don't think she sacrifices as much as my father does for my—all three of us on the whole. My father wouldn't care if—if the three of us, three of his sons, could be happy, my father would go live on a desert island right now if he really thought it would make us happier. Where my mother, I don't think she could really sacrifice like that. She said she would—she w—she would say she would. I think she honestly thinks she would. But from what I've seen of her, she has other uh other desires, like a new car and things like that. And if it works a little hardship on us as—as far as college money goes, then that's that. My father is always the one that's trying to hold down the budget for our sake. Things like that—My father definitely uh gives in to my mother quite a bit. That's the one person that he really does —is ruled by so to speak. He's not ruled by her. He's definitely the ruling person in our family. But as far as uh . . . whereas he won't take anything from anybody except my mother.

I:26 You mentioned the discussion of sex was a special taboo. Are there any others, particular to your mother?

S:26 Well, one thing is getting my father mad. She tries to present—prevent that whenever possible. Other taboos are things like uh (sniffs) anything which entails our really getting away for a long time, although she did not try to influence our choice of college. That was sort of out of her realm. She'd never been to college herself.

I:27 How does she feel about not having gone to college?

S:27 He's afraid he—she's afraid she might seem ignorant. Quite a lot of service women have not gone to college. They usually marry young and then they move, you know, and the women don't have a chance. On the whole that the—my mother has a very good time with the other officers' wives.

I:28 Are there any specific things that you feel that you got out of the relationship with your mother?

S:28 Yeah, one thing I think she definitely i-is a proposer of "Enjoy Life," as opposed to my father: "Do something in life; leave the world a little better for your having been here." So I've gotten a definite enjoyment in life. And I've gotten a . . . a definite uh . . . I don't know, there's a certain wonderful thing about my mother. I can't . . . I don't know exactly what it is. It's uh I guess it is that enjoy-life attitude basically more than anything else. . . .

I:29 Can you tell me something about your general physical health?

S:29 Well, I've never had any broken bones or any hospitalizations of any sort.

I:30 How do you sleep?

S:30 Well, I sleep well when I have a good bed. I'm not often awakened by uh noises and things like that. I can sleep—and I hardly ever dream.

I:31 How long will you lie around just before you fall off to sleep?

S:31 Well, I think quite a bit before I go to sleep—And so I'll maybe lay there for maybe twenty minutes; it doesn't bother me that I lay around awhile. And usually I think about relations with people, just for this uh—more or less on a psychological basis, try to think about my relations with my girl and my relations with people I've had dealings with that day and that sort of thing. And I often uh sort of in a dwa—daydream think about what's going to happen when I go back home this summer, how glad the girl will be to see you—you know, things like—envision the perfect set-up, things of that sort.

**I:32**   How about eating? What kind of an eater are you?

**S:32**   I eat m-meat, m-meat every day, say, in other words I-I-in a meal, I'm a—I don't eat a whole lot, but then I'm definitely not a light eater. But I eat to live sort of.

**I:33**   You usually eat a full breakfast?

**S:33**   Yeah, but before I came to Yale I didn't. See, before I came to Yale I had to make my own breakfast and my own lunch, my brothers and I all had to, because uh my mother would be-be-be sleeping. And my father would be off to work probably. So we'd come down in the morning and make our own breakfast. And there all's I did was to get by with the least amount of effort, just cold cereal and milk. And some fruit always. And then sandwiches for lunch every day. We had to make our own lunch.

**I:34**   How about constipation problems?

**S:34**   I wouldn't call it a problem, but my—like my father has told me I should make a habit of going right after breakfast every morning. But I just never formed that habit. So I don't know what—what time of the day I'm going to go or anything like that. But I don't—I don't—it's never been a problem to me, I just go when I have to. That might be twice in one day, one the next, or—

**I:35**   How about smoking?

**S:35**   I don't smoke. Oh, yes, I—when I was young, about twelve or thirteen. We'd smoke a few cigarettes but I never really had the—it was never really forbidden to me so I never really had the desire to run out and smoke, so I just never. Now and then at Yale I'll just pick up a cigarette, just to—And I don't want to start the habit.

**I:36**   Have you ever gotten any guff from other kids about not smoking?

**S:36**   No . . . The crowd I hung—I've been hanging around with doesn't really care about that, I don't think. At times, on a date, it's handy to be able to smoke, I'll-I'll have to admit that. When everyone else is lighting up and it has a certain sophisticated appeal about it. But that's the only time I've ever been tempted to want to smoke.

I:37 Do you smoke at those times?

S:37 No, I don't. Mainly because I think it would be rather foolish to put a cigarette in my mouth and not be able to inhale it. If I could inhale it, then I might do it, I admit.

I:38 How about drinking?

S:38 I drink, yes. I uh I don't drink a lot, drinking for pleasure more than anything el—I don't particularly like the taste of liquor. But if there's a wild party going on I'll be the first one to join in. But I don't do that to excess, I guess about maybe—I'll get high maybe once or twice a month. The only reason I do it is to have fun. If I've got a real good date I won't drink because I'll be interested enough in the date. But if I've got a poor date, and things are dead, then I can always have a good time when I'm high because—anything seems fun, anything seems funny.

I:39 Have you been active in athletic activities at any time?

S:39 Here at Yale: No. In my high school I was very active. I played uh football for three years. And I swim—swam for three years, baseball for two years, and basketball for two years.

I:40 How do you feel about your body as such?

S:40 Well, I like to keep a good trim body. I hate the idea of being fat. And that's why on my own I go up here to Yale quite often to do exercises in the—gymnastics, from push-ups, sit-ups, pull-ups. For no reason. It's just that I ff—get feeling uncomfortable and uh my mind punishes me whe—if I think I'm getting fat, or if I think I'm relaxing my physical condition. For some reason I just have that always over me that I have to keep in physical shape. I've often wondered why, but I don't. . . .

I:41 You say your mind punishes you.

S:41 Yeah, in other words, if we—I say it's always the—the tendency is to always get that extra hour of study in. And not go to the gym. But then a—I don't know, I just get feeling sl-sloppy I guess you'd call it. I get to feeling sort of like I'm getting fat and I can't stand the idea of being fat. So I go up there and work out real hard and—

I:42   How long have you felt this way?

S:42   Oh, I think for as long as I can remember. I've never—never liked fat women. And I don't like the idea of being fat myself. See, as long as I was real active in athletics I never had any worry about it. And always being on the beach a lot has a tendency to make you care for what your body looks like in itself. If you—I mean, you're in a bathing suit only, and if you have a fat stomach, and it doesn't look very good. So that—that in itself is a tendency to want to have a good looking body.

I:43   How do you feel about your body as far as that is concerned?

S.43   I think I've got a pretty good—pretty good build—pretty good body. I'm not ashamed to go around in a bathing suit or anything like that—

I:44   You mentioned your mind punishing you when you don't feel fit. Is this a real concern on your part would you say?

S:44   Well, it gets to be if I haven't gone up there for about two weeks. Then it becomes where I'm absolutely going to go up—next Monday. It mainly happens—no, I don't-I don't think think about it until I go to undress at night. And then I'll-I'll just uh—you know, taking off the clothing, you become aware of yourself. And uh then I'll start thinking how long I haven't been up there. Or my roommate will mention—my roommate loves to tease me about that also. This one roommate says, "Hey, you're getting fat, aren't you, Bill?" and yell something like that. He'll mean it jokingly but I'll just wonder, am I getting fat, you know, that—

I:45   Do you sort of examine yourself?

S:45   Yeah, in a sense, I do. I mean I don't stand in front of the mirror and flex for—at long periods enjoying my beautiful muscles. But I—in a sense do notice them—when I'm brushing my teeth or something, I just go in there with my pajama pants off and I'll see how I'm shaping up.

I:46   Do you have any feelings about your height?

S:46   Well, I wish I were taller. I wish I were about six feet.

I:47   How tall are you actually?

S:47  I'm about five-ten and three-quarters—five-eleven with shoes, but barefoot. I'd like to be about an inch and a half taller. But it doesn't bother me or anything.

I:48  Are you presently on a scholarship?

S:48  Yes, I am.

I:49  And do you do any work?

S:49  Dining hall—all freshmen have to do dining hall. Next year we get out of the dining hall and go into various activities.

I:50  Oh. How much time do you spend at that?

S:50  Every night for just about an hour and a half. And then three and a half hours on weekends or so.

I:51  How do you feel about this work?

S:51  It doesn't bother me. I feel I'd be wasting the time after dinner anyhow. The only time it really gets me mad is on the weekends, because I'm always trying to go away on weekends. And I'm always getting behind. And like last semester I lost six dollars, six hours worth because I couldn't make up my time. I was behind about forty hours. And I worked thirty-two hours the last week of exam week trying to make up. And I couldn't make it all up. I try not to have it limit me. An-and it still does limit me. As it is, I still have to stay here a lot of weekends that I wouldn't otherwise.

I:52  Are you the kind of a guy that's on time for the job?

S:52  I'm—I don't think I've ever been late except when it's essential to be. If I had a reading class from five to six I go to also, and that—I'm supposed to start work at six, so I get there five minutes late. And I'm not late otherwise.

I:53  How do you get along with your bosses or your boss?

S:53  Oh, fine. I mean, I'm known as a very, very lazy worker definitely. But they joke about it a lot. So that personally I get along with them great. But they're always joking about wanting to get rid of me. And I know they don't want to get rid of me really—I think they like me as a person. And I like them. But they do tease me about being a lazy worker and—

I:54  What do you mean by that?

S:54  I just don't move fast—I'm—I-I'm not—a lot of guys in there are hoping to get a bonus at the end of the year, so they give you a bonus if you're a real good worker. But I just don't see the point in knocking my brains out for that. So I go about my work at a steady rate. And I'm not going to get excited when the silverware runs out or something like that. Whereas with a lot of these people that work there, they get all—real nervous running around and all. I just don't—

**I:55**  How do you feel about working for some of the other students?

**S:55**  Oh, I don't mind that because a good deal of them are bursary boys themselves anyhow, a good deal of the upperclassmen. And I mean it's not looked at all degrading at Yale, so it doesn't bother me.

**I:56**  Have you held any other jobs before coming to Yale?

**S:56**  Summer jobs only. I've never worked during the year.

**I:57**  What kind of summer jobs?

**S:57**  Usually common labor. In my uh my soph—my junior year—my sopho—between my sophomore—no, between my junior and senior year was the first summer I worked. And that was uh as a common laborer up in Hawaii Dredging Company, making boxes, picking, shoveling, that sort of thing. And the next year I worked at a box factory in San Diego, California. Oh, and I had a paper route when I was a freshman and sophomore in high school in California. Every morning getting up at about six-thirty and delivering papers, but—and that was during the year—

**I:58**  During the summer did you work fulltime at these jobs?

**S:58**  Yeah, eight hours a day. Forty hour—common labor's type.

**I:59**  How do your parents feel about your working?

**S:59**  They definitely encourage it. I mean, they defin—they —it's the expected thing sort of, in the society I've been raised in. Everyone—everyone works like, during the summer. I don't mind it at all because if I start at seven I get out at four, and life is just beginning at four anyhow during the summer—

**I:60**  And what did you do with the money that you made?

**S:60**  I saved a good part of it. And that's what I'm—part of what I'm on at Yale right now. That's my money. I put it in the bank. And I've got some stock of my own.

**I:61**  That you bought with the money?

**S:61**  Yeah, my Dad—back when I was a freshman in high school, he gave us eight hundred dollars, and he said, "If you'll match this by the time you get out of high school, eight hundred, then I'll give you this eight hundred." So I matched it. I matched it with about a thousand, so I had about eighteen hundred to start college with. So I've had nine hundred of that in stocks, and I've spent a good deal of it now. And I've spent a lot last summer traveling.

I:62 And on these jobs how did you get along with the other workers?

S:62 Oh, fine. I think it's a refreshing change to get along with the common—Like the boss is practically the lowest type person I've ever seen in my life. Yy—as f—you know, I mean, they'd talk about nothing but wine, women, and song, day and night. But I like them—I like people like that for a change. I—enjoy—enjoy their company very much.

I:63 Did you feel you were accepted by them?

S:63 Yeah. As long as you give up all your ideas and—that you. . . . If you go in there with—and try to talk about it at noon hour your philosophies, then-then you wouldn't be. But if you go in there with them, and just listen to what they have to talk about and now and then add something, you get along swell with them. Try to talk on their plane, I mean, not that they're lower, but try to talk on things that would interest them, because they're not going to be interested in the stock market conditions or the economy of the United States.

I:64 Do you follow sports?

S:64 No, nothing bores me more than following sports—I-I don't read the newspaper to see what the New York Giants or anything like that is doing—I don't really follow the Yale sports, I just go to the games. I love games. I especially like hockey, football, and ba—and basketball. I really like ice hockey. I-I think it's the greatest sport I've ever seen in my life, fast and rough. I like that very much.

I:65 You enjoy fast, rough games.

S:65 Oh, yeah. The rougher the better. I—as far as I'm concerned the greatest game on earth would be no-no penalties—Just get out there on the ice and dive for it. (half-laugh) I like rough sports.

I:66 What kind of things do you do in your spare time?

S:66 I like music a lot. I have a—have—that's where a lot

of my money goes. I like classical and some complete rock 'n' roll.
I like things like—well, not real classical, I like *1812* Overture.
I like Beethoven. I like things like *William Tell* Overture, Sabre
Dance. I like those rather uh dramatic classical—I guess you'd
call them—and then I like complete rock 'n' roll sometimes. And
I like plain Doris Day type singing, vocal—

 **I:67** You say you buy records; how do you listen to them?

 **S:67** I have a phonograph.

 **I:68** And what do you do: for instance, do you have it on
while you work?

 **S:68** No, I don't usually listen to it while I'm studying.
When I'm writing letters I'll put on a lot of classical music.
That's when I like it. When you don't actually have to listen, but
it's pleasant to have it. And at times I'm just feeling in a certain
mood, I'll just come in and turn the phonograph on and lay
down on the bed and think with the thing real loud, or like
that, I sometimes do.

 **I:69** How about other things, other hobbies?

 **S:69** I don't really have uh—I indulge in politics in debating. I do that with the Union, Political Union. And I did that a
lot before in high school also. I-I enjoy that. When I'm actually
—I don't actually have much spare time at Yale. But when I
actually do I just either write letters or listen to music, or something like—something that I don't have to indulge in. I just like
to completely—to be doing something or completely doing nothing in a way sort of, I guess I don't—

 **I:70** Do you do any sort of extracurricular reading?

 **S:70** I try to but I don't really do any. I-I read on uh St.
Augustine now and then or some existentialism or Freud, but
I don't really go in for a regular plan of a book a week or any-
thing like that—

 **I:71** Did you use to read more?

 **S:71** Well, when I was in high school I had more free time,
and I read a lot of astronomy and a lot of Freud. But now I—
it's very rare that I get to because I have an extremely heavy
reading program.

 **I:72** How about novels or light reading or magazines?

 **S:72** No, I don't. I never read the newspaper hardly. I'll
read the *Yale Daily* but that's all. But I don't read *Time*. I'll look

at *Life* once in awhile, just look at the pictures, but I don't read that. And I won't read novels or anything like that, no.

**I:73**  You're interested in political matters and debating.

**S:73**  I'm interested in politics as far as it's concerned, the philosophy of politics—and the idea of either being the right or the liberal. But I'm not interested in United States politics as far as—whether the Republicans are going to come in or not, or anything like that. I don't follow that. I'm interested in the philosophy of it more than anything else.

**I:74**  Are you concerned at all about foreign policy?

**S:74**  I was, given up on that. I used to be very concerned and get very excited about whether the United States was . . . acting right. But I don't know, I've taken sort of a fatalistic at-titude. It more or less depresses me to think about how ridiculous our foreign policy is in a way. I fee—I've sort of accepted the philosophy of life where Rome rose and fell. I think America's going to rise abo—I just—sort of a cyclic theory—And I don't really see much point in . . . batting your brains out. Like I said before, I don't believe in God or anything, so I just believe I'm here for seventy years and then it's over. So I-I can't see going on a crusade. And I believe that all mankind is just here and then gone. And eventually, by believing the law of entropy I believe everything will be gone. So I can't see getting all excited about some puny thing like who's going to be ruling the earth more or less—and just so individual freedom can last, then I don't care really who's ruling.

**I:75**  You say that you felt our foreign policy was off-keel?

**S:75**  Well, like when I was down in South America, I mean the American—America always administers a policy on money basis. And we don't ever give the money to the people. In other words the European people themselves—never even know that America's giving money. That is ridiculous to pour in that amount of money and to have the people not even know it. The only ones that know it are the few top strata people in the state. They're the only ones that know it. And you can't—you can't buy that type of person anyhow. They'll sell out to the highest bidder. The friendship of the people can be helped by uh hospital type programs and real grass roots politics is what it's really called.

**I:76**  Do you feel that it makes any difference what party's in power?

**S:76**  Oh, yes, I definitely want the Republicans in power. I don't believe in the socialistic welfare state that I believe the Democrats are trying to work out. So I prefer the Republican and Conservative party to stay in and act as a brake on the ever-increasing socialistic trend.

**I:77**  Are you a hard studier? Do you work hard at studying?

**S:77**  Not particularly. I uh try to make studying too enjoyable, I think, most of the time. I've not yet resolved that studying is going to be a pain. I try to make it as enjoyable as possible. And therefore I'm probably not as efficient in my studying. Like last night, I just didn't feel like doing my chemistry, so I went to a movie.

**I:78**  Well, how have you made out so far?

**S:78**  I got an eighty average first term. I feel I'll make dean's list this next term, so I don't feel it's really hurting me. But I-I know I'm not brilliant. I think I have a natural ability for the sciences. Like my engineering comes almost naturally to me. And math, I can get a fairly decent grade, and chemistry I get a good grade. And they keep my average up. One—the few subjects I'm interested in like English and History are my lowest grades. And yet I can really get interested in these.

**I:79**  How do you explain this?

**S:79**  I tend to philosophize about it too much. And I don't hit the basic facts. And I'm always getting killed on who-said-such-and-such type questions. But if you could leave that aside and just talk in a general nature I think I really do well in History and English. I mean, for example, when I'm doing my math, chemistry, or engineering, I'll just do them and get them out of the way. I'll do the assignment, the minimum, and get them out of the way, and turn it in. Whereas with History and English I can actually think and-and wonder about it.

**I:80**  Is school something that you generally enjoy?

**S:80**  Yes. My life is always centered around the school. Especially in high school. My whole life was in the school there. But my life is never centered in my studies and I don't think there's really been any change here.

I:81  In general how are your relationships with girls, how do you see yourself?

S:81  Well, I . . . you mean how do I get along and how do they like me and that sort of thing? Well, I like girls very much. I like being around girls. And-and I get a very big kick out of it. I tend to make things too serious basically—and I think generally girls like me. But I tend to get too serious with girls. I tend to want them to like only—in other words, when I'm with them, them to see only me, and me be the center of attraction. And that's sort of a bad, selfish attitude to have and it only creates friction. But if I'm just going on a one-night date with a girl, I can—I can give her a really good time because I'm not really worried about getting real serious. But I start trying to get too deep and everything like that. And that sort of spoils it, after I've known the girl for say three months.

I:82  How do you feel with somebody that you've been going out with for awhile who also may be dating somebody else?

S:82  I don't like that at all. See, I won't stand for that. That's . . . completely out as far as I'm concerned. If I re—once get going with a girl and she's sort of my-girl type of affair, then—she's got to be only me and no one else. Well, in other words, I-I'm not meaning marriage or going steady. I've never done that. But I—when I say serious, I mean finding something —that girl should find something in me that she can't find in anybody else, and I should find something in her. In other words, she's supposed to be something special. I hate—to be thought of as just another date.

I:83  How about sexual experiences?

S:83  Oh, sort of light in a way. I've—I'm not—I'm not one that goes out on a date for sexual experience very much. So—I mean I've delved in it some, petting and things like that, but— I've never really gotten any sexual—really serious se-sexual experience with any girl. I've often thought about if I would if I had the chance. And I-I don't really know. I guess I'll have to wait until it happens.

I:84  You really have never had the chance in a sense.

S:84  Oh, I've had the chance. But I've just never had the desire. Definitely had the chance. One time I definitely had the chance to—have some good sex relations with a girl and I just had no desire to. It was out of a feeling of loyalty to this other girl that I was really going with at the time. See, it was a senior party and the girl I was going with was a sophomore. So she couldn't be there. And this other senior girl had been trying to seduce me you might put it. For about a year and a half. And she really tried that night. But uh it was more of a feeling of guilt if I had than anything. —Than anything else, I guess . . . so I've never really had anything.

I:85   Guilt towards the other girl?

S:85   I think—I think that's what it is. And yet often I wonder if it—is it really? I don't really know. I think—I th—on the surface it seems to be guilt out of . . . but in a—in a way I think it's something just general guilt toward sex. But when I—when I think of it I don't have any feelings of guilt toward sex, but yet deeply I think I do . . . In other words, if I look at it rationally in following my philosophy I have no qualms about having any sexual experiences with anyone. In other words, if I suddenly had the chance, I went up to Wellesley and there was this real good date, rationally out of my mind, I would have no problems about going anywhere with her because . . . I just—I have no religion to hold me back or anything like that. And yet if—when the time actually came, I-I wonder if I would because of my feelings that marriage is something special to me. And that it should be the first time that I ever do anything of that will be with my wife when I get married. In other words, I shouldn't delve in sexual intercourse until the time I'm actually married. And I'd want my wife to never have done it before with anyone else before me. So that would be the qualm that would be holding me back. And yet rationally I have no reason.

I:86   I wonder about a one-night date?

S:86   Well, they—there I'll get as far as I can sexually with them in a way, sort of. In other words, I wouldn't—I wouldn't want to have intercourse, but with a one-night date I'll pet and all that sort of stuff to see if—I'll—Sometimes I'll actually find myself making a contest to see how far I can get—which is a cruel thing to do to a girl. I don't do that often. But over Thanksgiving, I know, for example, at Rochester—that's another pressure that Yale's definitely put on me. In high school there was never that problem. But at college, especially being a Yale man, you've got a reputation for being a big lover. And you go out. And just by the very fact that you're in college and by the very fact that you're at Yale, you've got to do that. You have no choice. If you sit there all night and you try to talk philosophy to the girl or something, you'd be strictly a terrible date. So social pressures often make you have to do it; whether I'm in the mood or not, I've often got to play the part of the lover. But this one time at Rochester I found myself actually making a contest of it. And it got me very mad and it was against everything I believed in life to do something like that.

I:87 When would you say there were social pressures?

S:87 Well, if the girl goes out with a Yale man so to speak, she's not expecting to—she expects you to be polite at all times. And yet she expects you when no one is looking so to speak, to be a real man, the-the—the idea they have—of a real man. That's-that's the conno—connotation that Yale men sort of gives. And so you have to sort of live up to this. So there's an automatic pressure on you there to be—to in-indulge in sex. In other words, to definitely play on sex when you're on a date, for the reason that Yale men are expected to do that, be a big drinker, be a big lover, that sort of thing.

I:88 How do you feel that your parents' attitude about sex has affected you?

S:88 I think they've made me more strict than most—toward sex. I don't think they've played down sex. They've played up love in a sense. Uh that is, they played up dates with girls, put it that way. Especially my father. He's always been one to encourage dating girls, to encourage that. But they've never been one to encourage sex with girls. My father I don't think would disapprove so much. I know my mother would, very definitely disapprove.

I:89 When were you first interested in girls?

S:89 Quite young—quite young—twelve and thirteen. We, you know—well, actually, interested in girls and I guess it was more an in-interest in something new that I'd never done. We'd play lights out and spin the bottle and—that sort of routine (half laughing). I got a really big charge at that time—But even then I know I got very serious with a girl, even at that age. I got very interested in this one girl and went with her for about a year and a half, never went steady or anything like that. She was just sort of—I was sort of her guy and she was my girl was the idea, even at that young age (clears throat).

I:90   Well, when you were serious about a girl did this mean that you wouldn't neck or pet with her?

S:90   Well, I've often thought about that, yes. I've often thought about that. The girl I am serious with is the one who I won't neck or pet with. And yet that's not true, because the girl I'm most serious with in San Francisco I do neck and pet with her a lot. But before her it was definitely, I think, I had the girls I necked and pet with and the girls I was serious about. And they were two different . . . sta—but now they're being put into one more or less. . . .

I:91   Will you sort of heed a girl's no's about necking or petting?

S:91   You mean she says "No?" Oh, yes, I'm very sensitive to that. I wouldn't want to cause any conflict. A girl ever said "No" to me I just (snaps finger) . . . I'll stop. I'd never want to get into a fight or—or anything like that with a girl, I believe— It's ss—it's supremely embarrassing as far as I'm concerned and totally undesirable.

I:92   You don't push yourself.

S:92   No. Well, I do. If she says "No" the first time, you naturally—she just has to say that. So I understand that as far as her upbringing, I'll try again. But if she says "No" twice, then you know the girl means it. And so I'll stop right then. . . .

I:93   Do you feel that you will avoid having intercourse until you are married?

S:93   I think I will—in a sense, yes. In other words, I don't think I ever could go out seeking it. I've often wondered, like I—like I say, if the opportunity ever came, I think I would actually indulge in it. I'm not sure. I won't actually know, I don't think, until the time comes.

I:94   Do you have any particular thoughts about the kind of girl that you would want to marry?

S:94   Yes, she's got to be intelligent. I've often thought I wanted the other—I-I've often thought—that's something that came over me at Yale. I thought before I came to Yale that I wanted an ignorant wife, so to speak, so I would be undisputed master of the brain trust in the family. But I've completely changed my opinion there. I feel I would detest a dumb wife. She's got to be—got to give me some good idea—and I like more and more all the time the girls I take out around Yale. The sharper they are and the more witty they are the better I like them. So she'd have to have that. And she'd have to be very— she'd have to be completely devoted to me, my wife would, I think. . . . But the first thing to even get started, they have to be good looking. I mean, I can't stand a bad looking woman. For some reason they just—that's when I'll get—if I take a blind date and that will—the girl's really ugly, that's when I'll get high. I mean, and just forget about her. I just can't stand that.

**I:95** Do you have anybody in mind now as far as marriage is concerned?

**S:95** I'm thinking about this girl in San Francisco. But uh I don't really know. I think sh-sh . . . I-I think I love her in a way and I think she loves me in a way. But yet I can think of a lot of other girls I actually like better as girls. But yet she has a certain attraction to me these other ones don't have although they may be nicer, although they may be better looking.

**I:96** Do you have any idea what brought about this change from the ignorant wife to the intelligent one?

**S:96** I think a—I think I'd always been with intelligent wives—I mean, intelligent girls, excuse me—all the time. I've always been dating intelligent girls just because those were the girls I went around with. And so I always thought it would— how nice it would be if I could be—and I've never been total master. That's another thing. The girl was—that I become total master of I sort of lose interest in. The girls I keep interested in longest uh keep me hanging, so to speak, that I never become total master. So I think I set up this myth, this idea of an ignorant woman, and the idea that she would let me be total master, how nice that would be. But then when I came to Yale I ran into a lot of these dopey ones on blind dates. And then I just saw that's anything but what I wanted.

**I:97** What kind of things do you enjoy doing together?

**S:97** Oh, it can be anything. Going to a beach with girls and boys and sitting around—or sometimes just going and parking with a girl, or sometimes going to a hockey match or tonight'll be a formal prom. I mean—I can do just about anything with a girl that I do with a boy. Talk philosophy. Sometimes I'll go out with a date with my girl and do nothing but talk about philosophy all night.

I:98    Well, let's switch over to yourself. I wonder what kind of ambitions you have for yourself?

S:98    None except lead a happy life. I don't want to leave anything to the world really. My only fear is dying at a young age for some worthless purpose. And I consider dying for anything practically a worthless purpose. That's my only fear, that I won't be able to live life. I have this—always this stigma in my mind that says I've got to live life, keep living life while you're young, while you're young enough to enjoy it. So I can force myself to go out and experience life. A—and in that sense my ambition is really just to keep on, experience life in all its forms . . . happiness sometimes, sad at others, travel—

I:99    Well, aside from giving your life for a cause at an early age, do you have concerns about dying early?

S:99    Just that I—uh just that I would miss life. In other words, I know it's all over, just for me. It's all over, there's no God, no after life or anything like that. It's just over when I'm dead. And to me that's the greatest tragedy in the world. For say maybe to be crossing the street and get run over by a car. Because if—if I believe in God, I'd always have this afterlife if I'd lived a good life and that. But for me it's completely over— I'm not really anxious, but a young death just appalls me because I wouldn't be able to experience life and all the wonders of life and wonders of love and travel and happiness that—that are available in this world.

I:100    Do you worry about dying early?

S:100    No, I don't really worry about it—in fact, I'm very reckless sometimes, like when I get into a car, I just . . . sometimes, I mean, sit next to me and say, "Bill, keep your eyes on the road," all the time. And I mean I don't show off and hot rod that way. I just have no concern.

I:101    How about the kind of work you'd like to do.

S:101    I don't really know, and that's the—I was thinking at the end of this freshman year about going into the army for a couple of years, simply to mark time, to try to find out what I want to do so I can get in the proper major, I think, because I don't know what I want to do. No job appeals to me really. I've often thought about just going on to—living on a South Pacific island or wasting away my life. And I—if I could—If I—if I thought that were really happiness, I wouldn't hesitate a minute, I'd go. But I don't think that would be, I don't think that would be lasting happiness. I think I'd get bored with it. But I can just find a key to what would be happiness for myself, and I wouldn't hesitate a minute. I'd get out of college, I'd do anything just to—to find that happiness. I have love as a definite method of happiness. And I find that uh if I can get the proper wife and myself, I don't really care. If I could get my wife, myself, travel, good friends, and just keep moving all through life. If I had unlimited money, I'd never get a job. Just keep reading about philosophy that I enjoy and just keep . . . experiencing life, I guess is how you put it.

I:102   I wonder what you might have considered as possibilities?

S:102   Well, I've considered teaching because I uh enjoy uh putting my thoughts over to others. I considered big business simply for the money angle, that I could travel with a lot of money. So I have a conflicting desire, considered well paying jobs for the money of them but I wouldn't enjoy them so much. And I've considered low paying jobs that I could actually I think enjoy, in a sense, like a forest ranger or a teacher . . . often or something like that. Forest ranger because it's outdoors and out with nature and a teacher because it's dealing with people and I like dealing with people. . . . So I've thought about both these kinds of jobs and I really don't know what I want to do.

I:103   Well, at what point do you think you might have some idea?

S:103   I don't know. I wish I did know. Maybe it will be when I go through college. And I—I fear I might waste college. That's another fear of mine, that I might go through four years and waste my college education, not knowing what I want to do. . . .

I:104   What is the kind of thing you would definitely not want to be or do or be like?

S:104   I definitely would not want to be a draftsman, mechanic, or any—anything clerical, anything mechanical, hopeless like that. I want to deal with ideas or people or something dynamic. And I'd hate being a—working a typewriter or working a drafting set or—and I detest that. And really being an engineer appalls me. And yet I'm in engineering, of all the ridiculous things.

**I:105**   Well, what would you say about yourself as you are now, that you dislike?

**S:105**   Well, I just—I tend to think I'm awfully selfish. And I dislike that very much. I tend to think that I'm often using people for my own aims, I tend to think that I—I often wonder if I—if I really do love this girl in California, if it's really love or if it's just a—if she's just fulfilling something in me that I want to be fulfilled, and if it's purely ff—a "me-me" relationship or if it's really a "we" relationship. I tend to worry about that very much. I tend to worry that I'm too—worried about social pressures. I don't like that. I tend to try to be more individualistic and yet when I really analyze it I'm not so individualistic as I think I am a lot of times. I don't like that. And I don't like having to worry about monetary matters to an extent. And I don't like worrying in general and yet I do worry in general. I—I—I think I think too much sometimes. I often ss—want to just stop worrying about people, what people think of me, I th—I think I'm too egotistical in a sense.

**I:106**   And what would you say are the things you like particularly well about yourself?

**S:106**   (Clears throat) Uh particularly well abou—what I like about myself. . . . The thing that satisfies me about myself is my—my . . . my love of life, very happy with tha—I definitely do love life. A lot of people are existing in the world, but they don't really enjoy it. And then if they're existing, they're not living. And I definitely think I try to live a lot of experiences that other people miss. I like that about myself. And I like . . . uh about myself that I can uh . . . can love, at least try to love . . . And I like in general the way I—I like my position in life, being at Yale, having reasonable—I'm not poor, I'm not rich, but I'm not real poor, so—and I—and I'm very thankful for that. And I like—the thing—the main thing I like about myself really is that my future is in no way out, that I can always—and the thing

I like about myself, I think I'll have courage to do what I want to do. I hope that I won't go into a job for money reasons if I— if it won't make me happy. And I think I do have courage to do that. I think I have the courage to be something, just up and quit (snaps fingers), like the end of this year if I decide I want to go into the army for two years, I think I have the courage to make the definite step. I don't think I'm held down by things in life that a lot of people are. I can make new actions, accept new ideas, and suddenly take a whole radical course, it doesn't bother me in the slightest. In fact, I enjoy doing that. The out of the ordinary, so to speak. . . . And I like my—I ha-have a definite ability to get along with other people. I mean I always get mixed well with other people . . . I like that. . . . That's about all, I guess.

I:107   Are there any particular fears that you have about yourself?

S:107   Yes. One major fear is that I am going to go into the wrong thing for the wrong reason—the wrong job for the wrong reason. That's a definite fear . . . that I might get pressured into accepting a high paying job, that I might—I fear that I may become too conservative in my old age and be willing to put up with things that I would never put up with at this moment (clears throat). In other words, the wrong job or a . . . uh I'll just put up with life. And I never want to put up with life. I always want to live it and try to get something out of it. And I'm afraid that —I'm afraid that I'll become too conservative is the idea . . . and that's the only real fear I have actually. . . .

I:108   Can you tell me something about your standing in your own group of fellows at college? You mentioned at high school you were a leader.

S:108   Yeah, I'm usually the—one of the leaders, to put it frankly. I'm usually one of the—not one of the leaders always the one that's in the topmost position, but I'm usually one who is—is looked up to as far as being able to express opinions go. And I like that position. But I also like to not be in a position of being the head of the group. I was in the position of being the head of the group in Hawaii as president. And I didn't like that at all. Because then I couldn't communicate with people on the level that I wanted to. So I like to be in a position of respect and I like to be in a position of subordination at the same time. I like to be able to really talk to people as—as a real—real friend. And—and you can't often do that when you are in a position of elevation above others. You can't really get that communication.

I:109   In the follower-leader continuum, where would you place yourself?

S:109   I'd place myself as a leader. I think my talking has made a lot of people make decisions . . . and uh I think other people's talking made me a lot of—made me make a lot of decisions too, though, so it's—But I think I tend to change other people's more than they tend to change mine.

I:110   You don't like to be sort of *the* dominant figure?

S:110   Well, I do in a sense, but not in . . . no, because when you become the dominant figure you've lost all "we" relationship. It's—everything is you giving, and I like to receive, too. And I don't want to be receiving everything. I like to give too. So I like to be a definite "we" relationship.

I:111   Do you have strong feelings of like and dislike for people?

S:111   Oftentimes if I dislike someone I dislike them very intensely, yes. And when I like them . . . well, I wouldn't . . . I don't think they're too strong, but I think they're—well, I don't know exactly how you put this. I have a definite tendency to uh alienate myself very definitely with certain people. I've had this general tendency to try to like everybody and try to make everybody like me. So in other words, I can't alienate them completely because I'm still trying to make them like me no matter how much I hate them. Sometimes my roommate and I who are very good friends, I . . . I we definitely really get mad at each other —very, very heated, but I'll always make up.

I:112   I wonder if you have any feelings about how people should ideally be like?

S:112   Yeah, I've seen one ideal person really. That's a girl, I mean, out in Hawaii, she's going with my brother right now in California. She's—they—they may get married very definitely, I don't know if they will or not. But she's—she's to me almost the ideal person. She's intelligent. She's good looking, she's frivolous, carefree, very happy, enjoys life very much, is not intelligent in making good grades. She gets about a C average and yet she's sharp in the mind. She can discuss philosophically. She's aware of why she's living it. She's completely devoted to my brother, for example, or to whoever it is she happens to be loving, completely friendly to all people however. She's just a bubbling personality. I mean, she's—she's the . . . and yet she can be definitely dreary at times too. So she's not just one of these little on-the-surface, you find, little party dolls that are always smiling and running around. She's not that—those—I detest that type of person. She's —she's about as close to ideal as I've ever seen. I don't think I've ever seen the ideal person in a male, really. No—no—no man or any one of the male sex has ever struck me as ideal actually.

**I:113** Do you have any idea what you might be like five years from now?

**S:113** I think I'm basically going to be the same as I am now. I think I've been changing a lot. I think I'll definitely change. But I think my major period of change is over, at least I feel it is. I feel it has—I've gone through a lot of change just before college. And while—in my freshman year here I'm going through a lot. And I definitely feel I'll be changing through college. But I don't think—my basic ideas I don't think are going to change. I'm perfectly willing to let them if they want to, but I just don't think they will.

**I:114** How about socially five years from now?

**S:114** You mean where I'll stand i-i-in relation to others or— Socially five years from now. Well, I-I don't think I'll be at the top of anything. I don't think I'll be one of the real people that are in society or anything. I think I'll probably just be a . . . uh starting out. But I think I'll always have my basic good friends. The ones that really count to me. And I don't think I'll ever be one to ever be socially acceptable as far as society is concerned, wear the proper clothes and all that.

**I:115** Married?

**S:115** I don't think so. I don't think I'll get married for at least four years—three years, my remaining three years in college and probably three years after that. I'll probably be single for six years as far as I know.

**I:116** Well, going a little further ahead, how about twenty years from now?

**S:116** Well, I'll either be—there, see, there's where I don't know. I'll either be one of two things; and at any rate I'll be married in either case. And I'll either be a very happy person with no social foundation living a sort of tenuous existence . . . or not necessarily tenuous, but traveling I hope or uh in a low-paying job, but happy with my wife. Or I think I'll be . . . the alternative that I'm afraid will happen, I be—I'll be a social success and I'll be in a good job making money, living in a house, going to the office, coming home, kissing the wife, reading the paper, going to bed, that sort of routine. This mass uh mass executive type that America tends to turn out. So I think I'll be one of the two. I hope it will be the former. But I don't really know. It will be one of these two, I think.

I:117    How many children?

S:117    Three, about three, four maybe. Probably three, I guess. I say three because I come from a three-child family, but . . . three I guess.

I:118    How will you feel about sex life twenty years from now?

S:118    I don't think it will be as important to me. But I hope to never let it die because I feel it's a very essential part of marriage. But I don't feel I'll be as actively sexually as I am now naturally or as active as I will after marriage. But I hope to always keep—at least always, I say, up until I'm totally senile, sort of, and uh . . . and uh the—then all sex relations cease between a husband and wife at old age if they ever do.

I:119    How about your income in five and in twenty years?

S:119    In five years I think I'll be very poor, not very poor, but I don't think—I'm definitely not starting for money in a hurry. Maybe . . . five thousand in a year, say, four thousand a year. Uh twenty years from now? I'd actually guess my income would be twenty years from now . . . maybe . . . twenty-five thousand, thirty thousand dollars. That's—I don't know why I have that idea, but I just have that idea that's what it's going to be . . . So. . . .

I:120    Doing what?

S:120    Probably being in business somewhere, either with my father and brother, or else having made a fortune somehow, either in a job or something, and then retire and just living off the rest of it.

I:121   What do you consider twenty years from now to be a minimum income to live on?

S:121   About thirty thousand dollars . . . if I'm in society. Now, you see, I—I could actually be happy on ten thousand if I were living down in South America somewhere, I could be happy on much less, see. But if I'm living in the States and if I'm cottoning to, you know, the United States way of living, then I think I'll need at least thirty or forty thousand to be happy.

I:122   If things were to go badly in some way in the future, what is the worst anticipation that you might have?

S:122   That my wife dies and that I . . . That would really be the worst thing for me, for my wife to die at a young age. But then again I could always marry again, so that isn't so black, but it would definitely be a blow to me when it happened. And that my uh . . . that America became a welfare state. And that . . . that I got caught in a rut of a job. Those are the three real anticipations that I have.

I:123   What if things went bad maritally—what would be the worst kind of thing, outside of death of your wife?

S:123   Well, in a way the—my—the death of my wife could not be the worst thing. To me the worst thing would be divorce or something like that. And just living on a sort of bachelor but married relationship. I—I'd rather have her, really love her, have her die through some tragedy, but know that I really loved her all along, and then marry someone else perhaps, than just to go along and break up, lose this idea I have of love and just be living a bachelor's existence. I mean, but a married—married bachelor's existence sort of. That to me is the worst.

I:124   What do you consider the future of the world?

S:124   Socialistic (half-laugh), very black really because—I feel that the world is losing the ability to make the individual able to be himself. Through communism, and America is heading in that direction. And I feel the world of the future is a mass-think, mass-dress, mass-act type thing, which I detest. And I feel eventually the future of the world is—is end. The world will end eventually, not for any reasons except entropy.

I:125   Are you concerned about war?

S:125   Not really. It doesn't bother me too much. I don't think we'll have another big destructive war killing everybody off. I think the Russians have—the Russians are people and they have enough sense to realize that—that would be rather ridiculous. No point in that.

I:126   What about economic future?

S:126   Socialism, communism—state-running, state-planning type of economics. I feel the individual—the individual's owning property is something of the past. . . . As much as I—I wouldn't like to—as much as I like to see that stay, but I feel that private property is going out the window, private industry, things like that.

I:127   Could you tell me in five minutes or so how you see yourself presently, sort of an overall view?

S:127   Well, I see myself as a uh . . . uh deep-thinking, intelligent, but not brilliant person, a—I see myself as an out of the ordinary person. I see myself as a questioning person, wondering person, insecure person. And yet I like that in a sense. I'm glad I'm not secure and in—in my station in life already secured. I see myself as somebody who definitely has to have the like of others to be happy, definitely has to have the approval of other people, and I see myself as someone who—who uh likes the female sex a lot. Who likes the male sex also, but I have a definite attraction to females that—a very strong attraction. I see myself as a uh college student that's uh can handle the work. I have no qualms about flunking out of college or anything like that . . . And uh . . . I see myself as a mentally, maturing, more or less mature, but able to change all the time. But uh . . . I'm definitely in a state right now of total in a way insecurity. I'm—I'm—I know what I want and yet I can't get it in a sense. I know what I want is happiness and yet I don't know how to find it. And so I see myself as in a way knowing what I want, but I see myself in a very tenuous position of not knowing how to get it or how to go about it. And I see myself in a position of being afraid that I'm going to be through pressures of various kinds, be ff—no uh uh the very thing that I want, happiness being taken away from me, through the fault of no one else's but my own, in—through yielding to pressures . . . Ss—in fact I see myself as rather secure to put it mildly . . . questioning and wondering. And yet I see myself as someone who uh who thinks uh I think I love this girl . . . very much and I think she means a lot to me and I think

I mean a lot to her. But I don't really know there. See, I don't really know anything when you come right down to it . . . And actually—I guess that's actually how I'd sum up myself right now. I have a lot of opinions, don't really know anything, except that happiness is my goal, and how to find it I don't know. I—I— the one thing I do think I know is there is no God, that there is no—nothing in life, nothing is going to come along to save me in life or nothing's going to ruin me either. It's going to be my own way I make my life, that's going to happen.

I:128  Do you have any questions you want to ask me?

S:128  Do you think that uh a person—by talking to you from what you—do you think that a person in my age or my . . . thing has the ability—has—has had the experience of loving someone, do you feel that people young can love in a sense, or do you feel that's irrespective of age and it's more of uh thing.

## DISCUSSION OF RATINGS

### A. Ideational Styles

#### 1. *Cognitive reactivity*, Rating: 3.5

The subject's production in the interview session shows that he expresses himself quite easily, that his thoughts flow fairly rapidly and spontaneously, and without noteworthy resistances. He changes topics and sequences of ideas on occasion quite flexibly but the coherence of his thoughts remains reasonably tight throughout. There are no signs of actual flightiness or looseness as would be required for higher ratings. The facility of his associative processes and of his expression becomes particularly apparent during the first fifteen minutes of the interview in which he is requested to give a free autobiographical sketch.

#### 2. *Originality*, Rating: 2

Whenever interview material is being rated one may utilize the subject's way of expressing himself as well as the content of the subject's statements. Our subject tends to stick to facts. In his fairly faithfully narrative style of expression there are few indications of real fantasy or of any very unusual, original, or more complex or creative elaborations. In the content of the interview he also emphasizes rather conventional interests, desires, and ambitions. Although he occasionally expresses a desire to live a unique, idiosyncratic, and unusual existence of travel, excitement, and happiness, it seems that the varieties of existence which he can conceive for himself are fairly limited. They seem to range just about between this happy, carefree tramp existence and the life of an upper-middle-class executive. The over-all number of topics he broaches throughout the interview is also quite limited. Regardless of the questions asked he tends to return to the same topics again and again.

### 3. *Abstractness,* Rating: 3.5

Relevant again are the formal qualities of the interview as well as its contents, particularly the subject's descriptions of his interests and of the qualities of his studies and work. In general it seems that the subject became neither overly involved in the description of minor aspects of his life nor did he seem to generalize a great deal. Most of the time he is quite hesitant to go beyond the most obvious and immediately perceivable facts but on occasion he makes minor generalizations. Thus, a rating of 3.5 is probably more appropriate than a rating of 3 or lower. When he takes a philosophical approach to things it is not loose or over-generalized to the point where it begins to be so nonspecific as to be meaningless.

### 4. *Lability,* Rating: 2.5

In his responses to the interview questions the subject shows a fair amount of activity and of drive of a particular sort. Often, and sometimes repetitively, he tries to drive home certain issues, such as how important it is to him to be happy in life, to be individual, and not to be a conformist. All of this seems clearly to have a certain affective quality. His cognitive functioning seems to be quite noticeably steered by the influence of such affective or motivational preoccupations. If there is a slight degree of lack of control, it is certainly not one that really disrupts an orderly form of functioning. A low rating of 2.5 would thus seem representative. Some of his statements, made in a minor key as it were, reflect also a somewhat sober and constrictive position: his sense of being limited in his actions particularly with girls, the general hesitation with regard to becoming erotically involved and sexually excited as reflected in his preference for spending an evening with his date talking about philosophy rather than necking or petting (statement 86).

### 5. *Attentiveness,* Rating: 3.5

Although in this interview record there is no evidence of major disregard of reality circumstances, we find it nevertheless somewhat insistently dominated by the subject's personal concerns. There is his almost propagandized orientation towards the pursuit of happiness, his preconceived notion about how to approach the other sex as well as his almost demonstrative and repeatedly emphasized lack of commitment to any particular goal at the present time. One may say that his personal preoccupations take a certain amount of precedence over his perceptions of the details in his environment or of the attributes of other people. Thus, a rating nearer the avoidance or the insensitivity end of the scale would seem appropriate. However, this insensitivity or the lack of attentiveness are not of such a major sort that a much higher rating is warranted.

### B. Prominent Affects

### 1. *Depression,* Rating: 2

When using the scales of the affect group it is important to remember that they refer to the subject's personally experienced or expressed affect and not to affective tones inferred by the observer. In the case of our subject we are struck by an almost conspicuous absence of depressive emotions from the interview record. Only very occasionally is the possibility of depressive affect mentioned. In the last part the subject tells us how important it is to him to be liked by other people. Even here, however, he seems to be more worried than depressed about being possibly disliked. The consistent emphasis on happiness seems significantly to be opposed to the presence of depressive affects and may indicate a denial of depression. But depression as such does not seem to enter the subject's personal experience (see statement 106: "The thing that satisfies me about myself is my, my . . . love of life, very happy with that I definitely do love life.").

### 2. *Guilt,* Rating: 2.5

Again there is a relative absence of statements reflecting a subjective sense of guilt from the interview record. When the subject describes infractions of rules, primarily of the ones established by father, he seems to be more concerned with fear and with the external results of any misdeeds than with any internal affects of guilt. The only explicit reference to guilt reflecting an experienced or expressed emotion is in statement 85 when he speaks about guilt over possible sexual misbehavior. Even there he seems to be only approaching the whole subject cautiously and to be thinking more about the possibility of feeling guilty than to be feeling a real sense of guilt. A rather low rating would thus seem appropriate. Not relevant to the rating but to speculations about the dynamics of the subject's guilt might be the observation that in his family it is the mother who holds the moralistic and asexual position, and that the sexual area is the only one in which any guilt is expressed by the subject.

### 3. *Affection and love,* Rating: 2.5

The interview is filled with comments about love and loving. The subject states that his major interest in life is to have a loving wife and that he expects love to play a major role in his life "until senility sets in." Much of this, however, has a very narcissistic quality. In fact, in statement 2 he makes a slip saying that with respect to love and to girls in general "I demand too much as far as total devotion to myself goes on their part." There seems to be little indication in the record that he can give of himself to any great extent. His involvement seems basically with himself and with what can be done for him. There are few signs of mutuality, of giving, and of accepting affection. Relevant is his saying that until recently he wanted to have a dumb wife in order to be himself master of the household. When he says he has changed his opinion, he ends his comment stating that his wife would have to be "very-completely devoted to me." His concern with the entire issue such as reflected in statement 128 would indicate some awareness of a relative lack of capacity for expressing emotions of affection and love. The fact that he is aware of such an inability and that he realizes the possibility of a different orientation does not in itself imply, however, that he is able to experience stronger feelings of this sort at the present time.

### 4. *Shame*, Rating: 1.5

Scrutinizing first the formal aspects of the interview we find the subject at times expressing attitudes of what normally would be socially a rather outrageous quality. He says without embarrassment that he is selfish and that he does not care to leave anything behind him in the world. In the context of his health habits he describes his custom of studying his own body in the mirror. Presumably being seen by others he flexes his muscles. To a degree this may be an adolescent form of over-reacting against feelings of modesty as well as a manifestation of genuine physical pride. Experiences and expressions of emotions of shame thus seem to be fairly minimal.

### 5. *Frustration and thwartedness, dissatisfaction*, Rating: 1.5

Frustration and dissatisfaction are almost conspicuously absent from the record. The subject states that he enjoys friends, girls, and competition. He feels that he has enough money and he seems to sense no particular problems with authorities or discipline. The only mild indications of dissatisfaction, leading to a rating of more than 1, are found in the area of his future plans. Corresponding to his subjectively felt lack of commitment he is unsure and somewhat worried about life and about his future. On the whole, however, frustration and dissatisfaction are by no means a major part of his experience.

A comment might be made about the fairly frequent indications of a probable underlying depression in the interview. They may be related to his apparent reluctance to commit himself or to attach himself to an object (such as a girl, a career, an ideology). He may well fear separation or losses which perhaps dynamically represent anticipated repetitions of the frequent uprooting experiences during his childhood. They may have taken place in the context of his father's military career. These dynamic issues, however, do not seem to rise into consciousness and therefore should not influence our rating on this variable.

### 6. *Elation,* Rating: 3.5

The subject's constant emphasis on what might almost be called an ideology of the happy life and his generally hedonistic orientation are relevant here. Concerning his work in the dining hall he mentions that he laughs and smiles and that he is usually cheerful in relation to other people. At times he seems to express an almost striking unconcern with the more sad or depressing aspects of himself, of situations or of others. A rating of 4 with its implication of at least partly inappropriate elatedness is perhaps just too high, although one feels tempted to give it. He expresses quite steadily the feeling that nothing can go wrong, that he is always in control of situations, that he will be able to do whatever he wants to do. If it is his decision to make a lot of money he will make a lot of money, and if he decides to find a low paying but exciting and interesting job, he will also succeed. Sometimes he almost seems to convey some feelings of grandiosity and omnipotence which would seem to contribute to the experience of elation.

### 7. *Anxiety,* Rating: 2

On the whole the subject's responses seem relatively free from expressions of anxiety. Some indications of anxiety seem to appear in the last part when the subject has the opportunity to inquire about the interview and about the research project in general. At that time he asks several questions about his own position as compared to other students of his age in a number of areas, particularly in those of religious views and of loving. In another place he indicates that he does worry about money. He also states that he does not like worrying "yet I do worry in general, and I sometimes think too much." Dynamically it would appear that most of his anxiety appears in the relation between his ego and his superego. He seems to be somewhat worried especially in sexual situations. He fears the possibility of offending a girl or of acting in a way which would make him feel guilty later. There seems to be less anxiety about impulses and affects as such. Anger appears to be expressed fairly freely at times; sexual impulses and feelings are fairly open at least on the verbal level. He describes no noteworthy indications of phobias or anxiety-motivated avoidances. One exception may express itself in his concern that he might be accidentally killed while still young, especially while driving fast. One may speculate about the presence of certain unconscious preoccupations with fate in the subject's case, perhaps along the lines of what in the literature is sometimes referred to as "fate neurosis."

### 8. *Hostility,* Rating: 3

The subject clearly indicates in a number of instances a certain freedom to express and to feel hostility or anger. When his father would punish him, he would get "mad" although wisdom forbade him to show it freely. He likes rough sports (65) and enjoys the aggressive, angry, and hostile components of competition. Near the end of the interview he describes how he is able to have arguments with his roommate in which he "definitely, really gets mad at the others" (111). On the other hand, the subject seems to show no undue touchiness or readiness to react with anger as would be represented in a rating of 4.

### C. Prominent Defenses

### 1. *Repression,* Rating: 2.5

Throughout the interview the subject shows considerable openness about a variety of experiences and feelings including those concerning himself. As mentioned previously, he speaks freely about his muscle flexing and his interest in his body. He talks quite openly about his relationships to girls, to his family, and particularly to his mother. He responds to most questions with some freedom; fantasy seems to be the only somewhat restricted and circumscribed area. When asked about fantasies he sticks rather closely to the concrete aspects of the question, and seems incapable of going beyond it.

## 2. *Denial,* Rating: 4

Throughout the interview we see a domination of defensive denial. It clearly seems to outweigh any of the other defensive operations. The intensity of his denying leads to mildly hypomanic results: to an elevation of mood and a moderately Pollyannish orientation. He emphasizes that everything will always turn out well. Any kind of depressive affect, mood, or outlook upon the world seems to be particularly strongly denied. Possibilities of unhappiness, danger, or misfortune are especially minimized. This seems at times to reach such degrees that mild reality distortions, some insensitivity, or disregard of certain aspects of the self, of other people, and of the world result. The fact that almost all of the Prominent Affects except elation received rather low ratings reflects the effect of the subject's tendency to deny. His tendency to deny remained quite persistent through the interview as it seems to do in his life. There are only rare instances in which the denial breaks down and the content of what is denied comes through.

## 3. *Projection,* Rating: 1.5

The record on the whole is marked by a rather high degree of aloofness and by the relative lack of feelings and ideas concerning others. The subject is quite self-centered. There is a strongly held assumption that relations with others are all right and that he will always be liked. It seems almost as if the pervasive defensive denial overrides the subject's possibilities for projection. There is even less projection indicated in the interview record than might be useful for adaptive purposes. Although some of the indicated wishes for dependable external authorities, to assist in the maintenance of self-discipline, might appear to look like projected superego-components, it seems more accurate to interpret them as indications of a relatively poor and underdeveloped integration of his superego with the rest of his ego. There seems also to be no significant manifestation of projected drive contents.

### 4. Reaction formation, Rating: 2

There is not much evidence that reaction formations represent a major form of defense in this subject. There are no expressions of "slovenly, smutty, or cruel" patterns in the material, nor is there much emphasis on the overly considerate or excessively clean or nonaggressive traits which would exemplify the effect of such defenses.

### 5. Isolation, Rating: 2

While the subject does show a certain tendency to avoid the affects appropriate to various situations (especially depressive affects) this appears to represent the workings of denial much more than those of isolation. The aim of his defensive operations is not so much the elimination of affects which would be consistent with the presence of isolating tendencies, but it seems to be more the substitution of other affects in place of the original ones. There is sufficient evidence of an emphasis on emotionally neutral intellectual and cognitive functions to make an "ordinary" rating of isolation appropriate. A higher rating, however, would be inapplicable.

### 6. Intellectualization, Rating: 1.5

The subject not only shows little intellectualization but he almost goes out of his way to avoid intellectuality. Statement 72, concerning his reading habits, tells us that he hardly reads the daily newspaper and in general nothing besides required material. In other places he states that he avoids scrutinizing the details of politics and that he is satisfied with a general and unelaborated liberalistic philosophy. In reference to studying (77) he indicates that he wants to make it enjoyable; he underplays the intellectual effort. A hedonistic pursuit of the joy of life and an avoidance of serious intellectual scrutiny of almost anything characterize his orientation to the world. When asked about his conception of an ideal person he answers that it would be a girl (since he cannot think of a man as an ideal). His description of her is that "she's intelligent, she's good looking, she's frivolous, carefree, very happy, enjoys life very much, is not intelligent in making good grades; she gets about a C average and yet she is sharp in the mind . . ." (112).

### 7. *Rationalization,* Rating: 2.5

There are only few observable instances of rationalization in the interview record. Those that occur are less in terms of common sense or utilitarian justifications but more in terms of the subject's general happiness-philosophy; they also serve the support of his parents' policies and outlooks. The rarity of instances of rationalization might lead to a rating of "cannot say" as easily as to a low rating on the scale. This subject's rating on the defense of rationalization is thus somewhat weak and uncertain.

### 8. *Undoing,* Rating: 1

No instances of undoing are observable in the interview record, nor are any practices that might involve undoing reported by the subject.

### 9. *Introjection and identification*

a. *With aggressor,* Rating: 2.   Evidence relevant to this rating may be found in the subject's descriptions of his father as a forceful and self-righteous man, who especially in his own college days has been enterprising, active, and wild. The subject does not indicate a sense of identification with his father in these terms; on the contrary he seems to hold himself somewhat away from such a position. Rather, he mentions some fear of the father, for instance in the episode of father's warnings against catching VD. On the other hand, there seems to be altogether no emphasis on victimization in the record. Relevant in this context may also be the subject's rather counterphobically tinged, dangerous driving habits as well as his fear that he might die young. It seems as if he were testing out this fear and also, possibly, the degree and danger of some aggression turned against his own self. But the exact nature of this trend is unclear. The previously mentioned indications of some mildly feminine identification trends such as found in the subject's concern with his own body and with being the center of attraction would also speak against any major identification with an aggressor.

b. *Altruistic*, Rating: 2.5. There are occasional signs of altruistic trends. One of them might be the subject's participation in the research project itself. He is willing to give considerable amounts of information, even about uncomfortable topics. Relevant also may be his reluctance to go too far with girls for fear of hurting them. While some anxieties may contribute to such behavior, it probably has some empathic, altruistic aspects also. In statement 110, when asked about wanting to be a dominant figure, he says: "Well, I do in a sense, but not in, no, because when you become the dominant figure you have lost all 'we' relationships, everything is you giving and I like to receive too, and I don't want to be receiving everything; I like to give too. I like to be in a definite 'we' relationship." This statement has some altruistic implications as has the next one to be cited. In statement 75 the subject expresses his desire for aid and assistance to the simple people in foreign countries, and he shows some fairly idealistic veneration for certain people who devote their lives to this kind of work.

## 10. *Over-all defensive success*, Rating: 3.5

At first one might lean towards a rating of 4. The subject's defenses, on the whole, seem to carry him through very well. The interview reflects neither extraordinary rigidity in his functioning nor are there intrusions of autistic ideas or other manifestations of the primary process. There are no signs of significantly idiosyncratic fantasies or inappropriate affective responses. On the other hand, there is a mild degree of constriction in his functioning due to the intensity of his denial. The effects of this defense reduce the variety and richness of the subject's responses both intellectually and emotionally. Consequently, a rating towards only "moderately successful" is appropriate.

## D. Superego

### 1. *Severity*, Rating: 2.5

There are no major expressions of superego severity in this record. Some guilt feelings are present with regard to sex but outside of this area not much guilt can be observed or inferred from the interview contents. On the contrary, he expresses almost exaggerated self-esteem; there is a lack of any sense of failure, and there is no noteworthy amount of self-derogation. When he discusses the way in which he desires women to act towards him or that he is an atheist, or when he describes his attitude towards his bursary work, he makes these socially not necessarily acceptable statements with great freedom and self-confidence. His emphasis on enjoying life and his lack of perceiving any need for working, except to obtain money when necessary, also are not hallmarks of a very guilt-ridden individual.

### 2. *Integration*, Rating: 2

Evidence requiring us to infer an only partial integration of his superego with the rest of his ego functioning can be found in several instances. In statement 59 the subject expresses a wish for externally imposed discipline. In statements 10 and 11 he talks at some length about a double standard concerning swearing. At home swearing is forbidden, and the subject realizes the moral justification of this prohibition. But when away from home he feels free to swear as much as he wants. Also, concerning the previously discussed sexual guilt there are some indications of his being more worried about incurring dislike or disaffection from a girl than about the moral issue as such. His pursuit of happiness may also often be guided more by the possibility of gratification than by consistent and autonomous moral standards.

## E. Adaptive Strengths

### 1. *Adequacy of reality testing,* Rating: 3.5

In general the subject's reality contact seems to be quite good. In describing the parental figures, for instance, he expresses a fairly broad range of observations, both favorable and unfavorable, with a certain degree of subtlety. In his sensitivity towards even minor traits of his parents' personalities, but also in his perceptions of the world and its future, or of the requirements of college and of work we find a reasonably comprehensive view of reality. The half-point deviation of the rating given from the optimal rating appears justified because the heavy reliance on denial seems at times to lead to insufficient appreciation of less favorable or pleasant aspects of his own self or of situations. The relative lack of depth in his thinking, which will be expressed in an appropriate rating later, also contributes to a mild lack of attunedness of his cognitive processes to the conditions surrounding him or prevailing within him.

### 2. *Degree of synthesis within the ego,* Rating 2.5

The interview record contains some significant manifestations of lacking integration between various features of the subject's ego functioning. For instance, in describing his political position he professes conservative Republicanism but subsequently he states that he wants to be free to do radical things and that he fears becoming a conservative (107). Similarly, while he generally advocates a democratic position, he feels strongly that he is superior to women, and he insists repeatedly that his wife or any girl that he might go with has to be totally devoted to him. His vocational plans, including the careers of forest ranger, teacher, or big business executive, seem also fairly divergent. His lack of knowledge of where he is going is reflected in statement 101: "I don't really know, and that's the—I was thinking at the end of this freshman year about going into the army for a couple of years simply to mark time, to try and find out what I want to do, so I can get into the proper major. I think because

I don't know what I want to do no job appeals to me really."
He also says that he has often thought of just staying on a South
Pacific island and wasting away his life. "If I thought there were
real happiness I wouldn't hesitate a minute, I'd go."

### 3. *Stress tolerance,* Rating: 4

There is little evidence concerning this variable either in the
form or the content of the interview. The subject has not reported any noteworthy stresses to which he has so far been
exposed. Although he mentions frequent moves, especially during
his early years, he indicates at least no conscious difficulties in
adapting to new surroundings. He has, on the contrary, shown a
good deal of apparent independence in traveling around and in
undertaking various enterprises. Certainly in everyday situations
such as school, vacation, and in social relationships he seems
able to function without disruption. How he reacted to these
stresses unconsciously is another question. It seems suggested that
the frequent moves may have perhaps contributed to a certain
sense of rootlessness and to a basic fear of becoming involved.
These reactions, however, are to be encompassed in later ratings
concerning the character developments that may have derived
from them.

### 4. *Amount of committable energy available for adaptive tasks,* Rating: 3

The rating of "fair" on this dimension may not do justice to
the possibility that under pressure the subject may be capable of
sustained effort and considerable involvement. However, he indicates in the interview that his efforts and his interests in studying are limited. Similarly it seems that no job is of particular
interest to him and that he is rather unwilling to involve himself in any major tasks, or hobbies, or reading outside of what is
required. Although he states that he has been working a good
deal in his spare time and earning money, he also tells us that he
is considered lazy on the job and puts in as little effort as possible
without displeasing the boss.

## 5. *Strength and variety of experienced affects*

a. *Strength*, Rating: 3.5.   The subject describes fairly strong emotions and affects in several instances. He tells us that he can get angry and furious (8), about restlessness (3), of jealousy of his brother (24), and more about aggression and anger (65). Then there is the repeated emphasis on happiness which, however, often seems to be more of an ideology than an actually experienced affect although there are probably also feelings of happiness. Thus there is a reasonable amount of evidence that fairly strong emotions come to the surface at least at times, and fairly lively affective experience is apparently not foreign to the subject.

b. *Variety and complexity*, Rating: 2.5.   The variety and complexity of affects and emotions manifested in the interview are fairly limited. Descriptions of feelings are mostly restricted to "happiness" and anger. Occasionally he mentions also jealousy and fearfulness, and we may infer occasional experiences of lust. On the whole, however, his affective experience tends to be somewhat limited due to his defensive denial of unpleasant feelings and to his mildly indiscriminate emphasis on joyous and happy moods. With his constant attempt at a cheerful attitude he also seems to try to make everybody like him: "So in other words I can't alienate them completely because I'm still trying to make them like me no matter how much I hate them."

## 6. *Profundity and variety of thought contents*

a. *Profundity*, Rating: 2.   Throughout the interview the subject mostly describes actual events as well as certain attitudes and orientations but he does not go into their depths or implications. Fairly often he voices rather superficial opinions, for instance concerning politics or morality; but he seems to experience no need to generalize from them, to relate them to one another, or to doubt and examine them. Some exception to this may be found in his sometimes sensitive and detailed perceptions of certain other people. But on the whole there is little subtlety or differentiation to his thinking.

b. *Variety*, Rating: 2.5.   Some of the previously mentioned considerations apply again. The subject's tendency to deny, his happiness ideology, and his relative shallowness of thought dominate the picture. It even seems possible that the variety of information found in the interview record might have been less had the subject not been responding to a range of questions covering a variety of topics. His involvement with intellectual issues seems as limited as his range of ideas concerning extra-curricular activities or interests of his own.

### 7. Regression in the service of the ego

a. *Over-all rating*, Rating: 2.    Throughout the interview the subject remains essentially fairly factual. He says very little about any personal fantasy or about irrational concerns, symptoms, or experiences of any kind. There is little preoccupation with his own internal processes. They do not seem to occupy an important place in the perception of his own self. There are no significant signs of imagination, of originality, or of idiosyncratic or creative production. Even a rating of 2 is not entirely satisfactory since we find no instances of unwilling or surprised concern with internal experience. But a rating of 1 would clearly be too extreme.

b. *Creative output*, Rating: 1.5.    Throughout the interview the subject shows rather a lack of interest in anything creative or unique, in adding something new to the world in his lifetime, or in doing anything that is particularly worthwhile. He indicates that he reads only what is required and that he pursues no particular interests, outside studies, or hobbies. A rating of 1 would seem inappropriate for he is not a "machine-like" being but, on the other hand, there are no significant indications that even minor creativeness plays a role in his life.

c. *Wit, humor, and playfulness*, Rating: 1.5; 4.    The following considerations lead to a split rating. On the one hand, there is not much wit or humor in the subject's productions. He does not seem to produce much in the line of humorous twists, of anticlimactic statements, or of unusual and momentarily un-expected points of view. On the other hand, he shows some playfulness although one might ask whether his kind of playing is not perhaps fairly empty. It may well represent a kind of drifting more than a productive regression which results in taking into consciousness and in the utilization of previously unconscious ideas, fantasies, or feelings. The rating of 4, representing his playfulness should be seen as being closer to step 5 on the scale in which playfulness is represented in a form bordering on disorganization and on an inability to consolidate energies into more constructive channels.

## 8. Social adaptiveness

a. *Ability to change oneself (autoplastic)*, Rating: 4. Repeatedly the subject indicates considerable efforts on his part to be liked by others, to fit in, and to be one of the boys. Even while working he seems more involved in these efforts than in his job. His relative lack of self-definition and of commitment to any particular orientation, political, moral or otherwise, would further aid his self-modifying tendencies.

b. *Ability to change or influence others*, Rating: 3. Relevant here seem to be the subject's descriptions of having been elected president of his high school class or of his self-estimate as being more a leader than a follower. The importance, to him, of being liked, however, may prevent him from executing leadership responsibilities if they would tend to make him unpopular. He may also be somewhat uncomfortable in what he seems to feel as the isolation of the position of a leader. Nevertheless we find that in his last year of high school he became an officer in the ROTC and participated in the science club, the sabre and chain club, and the honor society.

c. *Flexibility of social exploration and affiliation*, Rating: 3.5 Not much is said in the interview about the subject's attempts to make new friends or other social contacts. This may be partly due to the fact that this interview was held early in his freshman year when he was still adapting to a new environment. He makes, however, some comments about the relative ease with which in the past he has made new contacts after his frequent moves. Thus, affiliation does not seem to be too much of a problem. On the other hand, there is little evidence of active social exploration nor does he seem to mention longer lasting social ties which are maintained despite geographical moves.

d. *State of social adaptation,* Rating: 3. Superficially it would appear that the subject is socially quite well adapted and that a higher rating would therefore be applicable. However, much of the pleasure in human relationships that is expressed by him in the interview seems to be rather narcissistic; his relationships seem to be only partly genuine. He consciously acknowledges a fair amount of selfishness; he onesidedly stresses girls' and womens' devotion to him; he desires to be catered to; and he actually points out that until recently he wished for a "dumb" wife to whom he could be master (94). On the other hand, there are also several indications that he does enjoy contacts with other people. In high school he was popular enough to be elected president of the student body; he was active in many clubs; he states openly that he wanted very much to be liked, and that leadership positions are difficult for him because in them he loses a "we" feeling. Among his professional choices is that of forest ranger. The wish for such an isolated job would somewhat counterindicate the presence of profound pleasure in human relations. His other choices of teacher or big businessman again imply social contacts. He also says that the idea of becoming an engineer appalls him (104); and he seems to show some increasing interest in the social sciences.

## 9. *Drive regulation, utilization, and implementation,* Rating: 3.5

The subject clearly at times experiences aggressive impulses, sexual drives, as well as certain states of excitement and restlessness. It appears that generally he is able to control and channel these impulses fairly well. In his sexual behavior, for instance, he shows that he not only is quite able to check impulses but even to inhibit them. On the whole it does not seem that he has had any noteworthy difficulties with the environment because of his impulses; there seems to be a fairly good capacity for fitting in; overall, as well as in terms of specific impulses. His capacity for enjoyment, however, appears to be mildly limited. Various inhibitions, the need to maintain certain defenses, and the underlying depressive orientation, all would counterindicate a higher rating.

## F. Sense of Self

### 1. *Control vs. being influenced,* Rating: $2_{3.5}$

In general the subject expresses a sense of being in command, in control of himself, and of running his affairs as well as his relationships with other people and with situations. His subjective sense of mastery is supported by his life history in which he seems to show fairly successful mastery up to the present. The subrating of 3.5 is given to represent a sense of being influenced which seems to prevail on more unconscious levels. He seems to feel himself to be somewhat at the mercy of external events such as the relatively frequent uprootings in the past, against which the subject was helpless, or in his relationship to his powerful, although superficially friendly and manageable father. His indecisiveness about the future and his future career also seems to contain a subjective sense of being somewhat adrift. This sense of being influenced, however, does not appear to reach the same intensity as the sense of being in control of his relationships.

### 2. *Involvement (active or passive) vs. detachment,* Rating: $4_2$

Although we have indications of occasional, relatively superficial, and temporary involvement in some areas, such as his high school activities, the ROTC, and various clubs, we are more consistently struck by the picture of detachment, of narcissism, and of relative emotional isolation. He is mainly interested in his own happiness, and he lacks a desire to leave anything behind or to make any contribution other than to his own comfort and enjoyment. This detachment appears not only in social relationships but also in intellectual activities. He invests little in school work, and maintains no discipline in his studies which he feels should be only enjoyable (77). The subrating of 2 is intended to reflect the occasional instances of involvement. They concern his attempts to enjoy life: he becomes somewhat involved in parties and in social activities (such as those in Brazil and Hawaii). But even here his involvement seems often quite thin; sometimes his participation in social life seems to be predominantly a status issue.

3. *Expansion of relations with the not-self vs. constriction*, Rating: 3

The record reflects no major expansive trend. This is apparent in a number of areas. Socially the subject seems to enter new relations as the opportunity arises but he does not seem to strive in any particular direction or to seek out actively a greater number of certain kinds of social contacts. The same seems to be true in the intellectual area: the subject seems to do what is necessary in his college work but not to pursue any interest or concerns of his own. This seems also true with regard to his future plans, to his philosophy of life, ideology, etc. On the other hand, there appears to be no significant evidence of any active constriction, or of attempts to abandon issues or concerns with which he has been involved up to the present time.

4. *Homogeneity of the self vs. conflict*, Rating: 3.5

On the whole the subject does not seem burdened by any particular or striking conflict but his over-all uncertainty, his sexual inhibitions, and his difficulties with values seem to betray a certain sense of unsettledness. Also from the intensity of his pursuit of happiness we may infer that the subject does not yet sense himself as having reached a prevailing state of satisfaction or contentment. A rating mildly on the side of internal conflict is therefore appropriate.

5. *Body image*, Rating: 2

A good deal of preoccupation with the body is expressed rather freely and openly in the interview. The subject describes his discomfort over becoming fat and feeling large and says that: "my mind punishes me if I think I'm getting fat." He talks about standing in front of the mirror checking his muscles and looking at his body generally, and he derives enjoyment from doing so. He remembers that when he was living in Hawaii he spent most of his time in a bathing suit and that he therefore put a good deal of effort into looking fit and well. There is further emphasis on training, on being athletic, and on looking trim. While ideally the subject would wish to be taller, he nevertheless seems to feel quite satisfied with his body in general.

### 6. *Acceptance of the self vs. rejection,* Rating: 3.5

The record on the whole is pervaded by statements, partly perhaps representing efforts at denial, indicating that the subject senses himself essentially as all right. Yet taking again into account some of the factors already discussed, such as his uncertainty about the future, his doubts concerning his own moral fibre, his concern with his own body, and others, it would appear that we should also infer at least a mild element of dissatisfaction with his own self. The dissatisfaction, however, does not seem to be sufficiently intense to motivate the subject towards any kind of program for self-improvement.

### G. Psychosocial Modalities

### A. *Subject's standing on each modality*

1. *Trust vs. basic mistrust, Rating* $2_{3.5}$. The subject's self-confidence, his general optimism, his anticipation of future happiness, however wishful it may be, his generally favorable orientation toward others, and his frequently expressed good will all would seem to be evidence of trust. The subrating of 3.5, on the other hand, is given to encompass some of the more underlying trends of mistrust which seem to include some basic frustrations of orality and of dependency, and some indications of covert depressive trends. We may also refer again to what may appear as a rather basic sense of uprootedness, and to the subject's deep reluctance to commit himself fully to another person, to any issue, or, so far, to any definite course in life.

2. *Autonomy vs. shame and doubt,* Rating: 2. Fairly frequently the subject indicates pride of his freedom and of his independence from home which, in fact, always seems to have been considerable. He does not indicate a need for much justification for conducting his life according to his own, mostly hedonistic, wishes. He exudes a certain air of self-confidence

which only at times is undercut by a mild, depressive tone. He feels that the choices ahead are his own, and that he will be able to make the necessary decisions when the time comes for them. He does not appear too concerned with orderliness, precision, or parsimony. It seems also significant, particularly in his relationship to his somewhat authoritarian father, that he appears to maintain a much less rebellious orientation than one of a reasonably comfortable freedom and independence.

3. *Initiative vs. guilt,* Rating: 3. The interview record suggests that the subject stands about midway between these poles. The subject shows a fair capacity for entering new undertakings, but this is mostly true when they are part of a fairly normal life routine. There are no signs of extraordinary initiative or unusual self-propulsion. On the other hand, some inhibitions of initiative, particularly in the areas of sex and of intellect, are indicated. Thus the subject describes his interest in "delving" sexually (83) but also his guilt, inhibitions, and qualms of conscience concerning such delving (85). A similar inhibition of intellectual "delving" seems to appear in the subject's almost anxious avoidance of any deep or detailed scrutiny of issues or problems of any kind. He much prefers to stay on the surface. All in all, however, neither initiative nor guilt seem to predominate greatly over the other.

4. *Industry vs. inferiority,* Rating: 3. In the present subject's case this rating is given with much uncertainty. A rating of X might well be more appropriate. As for industry, we find little evidence that this has ever been an issue of much importance in his life. He does not appear to have ever worked hard or to have pursued an interest or activity with any persistence. In some of his work situations, such as in the dining hall, he describes getting by on the basis of his charm so that he does not fail on the job although he may not be doing the work. Conversely, however, there is no evidence of any profound sense of inability, of lack of skill, of equipment, or anything of the sort. The subject is reasonably self-confident and optimistic concerning his capacity to cope.

At this point we may raise the question whether the subject has developed significantly beyond the psychosocial stage of initiative. We find in scrutinizing the record for evidence concerning the following stages that beginning with this issue of Industry vs. Inferiority each subsequent stage seems to be lacking relevant manifestations in the available data. It should be added that this is not usually true of interview records obtained from subjects of this age. It may well be that this subject has so far fairly much remained on the phallic, and perhaps narcissistic, level of development which corresponds psychosocially to the issue of initiative. With this in mind, we approach the following ratings with some reservations.

5. *Identity vs. identity diffusion,* Rating: 4.   Socially the subject shows a certain but perhaps superficial integration with the society of his peers which, however, may really be due to an ability to get along with others based on a relative lack of personal definition and commitment. Considering the subject's uncertain plans for the future, his lack of allegiance to any religious, philosophical, or political ideology, and his uncertainty as to the validity of moral standards, we must infer the presence of a fairly marked identity diffusion. A noteworthy lack of integration also appears in his opinions, and an equal unsettledness exists in relation to his own sexual and aggressive impulses whose place in his ego structure is still undefined. Occasional manifestations of oppositional or mildly negative identity features appear but not in major proportions. In line with our previous discussion, the possibility should be considered that the subject has not yet approached the issue of identity formation so that the present picture may be one more of immaturity than of diffusion.

6. *Intimacy vs. isolation,* Rating: 4.   Some of the preceding considerations can be similarly applied in this category. The interview record lacks descriptions of specifically mentioned personal friendships of any depth, although the subject's relationship to his brother may have something of such a quality. Nor does he describe deeper or more sensitive relationships with girls. He narcissistically wishes to be admired but there seems to be no significant degree of mutuality or emotional give-and-take. Even indications of intimate cooperativeness are lacking. Relevant to this issue, and reflecting possibly some beginning concerns with

this issue, are the subject's questions concerning his ability to love which appear near the end of the interview.

7. *Generativity vs. stagnation,* Rating: 4.5. In considering this dimension one must raise the issue of age-relevance. Erikson assigns the development of generativity to the earlier phases of mature adulthood. Merely chronologically our subject would not be expected to have reached a level in which this issue is clearly prominent. Therefore one might agree to a convention of assigning ratings of X to subjects of such an age group. In the interest of demonstrating the rating procedure, however, we decided to assign a rating. Relevant would seem to be the subject's active and almost demonstrative avoidance of making contributions to the world, to other people, or of leaving anything behind him when he dies. To a degree this may also be an expression of some of the previously mentioned mild trends of negative identity. Be that as it may, the subject so far has not shown active interest in any kind of creation, in making contributions, or especially, in having children or rearing them.

## B. *Degree of emphasis of each modality*

1. *Trust vs. basic mistrust,* Rating: 1.5. Not much concern with the entire issue of trust vs. mistrust can be found in this interview. Perhaps the lack of such concerns is in itself an expression of a relatively trustful orientation. On the whole the subject seems to take his relations to himself and to the world quite for granted, whatever they are. Although the previously mentioned conflict between wishes to come close to people and his hesitation to make commitments is somewhat relevant here, it appears nevertheless that this ambivalence is expressed less in terms of trust or mistrust and more in terms of some of the later issues. As we see the subject at the present time, then, there is no immediate major emphasis on this modality.

2. *Autonomy vs. shame and doubt,* Rating: 3. Relevant to this issue are some of the comments made by the subject concerning the freedom with which he, as well as his brothers, were allowed to do various things, and what he says about his reac-

tions to rules and proscriptions in general. We previously discussed the observation that the subject's superego standards appear so far to be only partly integrated with his ego functioning and that, in many instances, he still seems to try to define the degree and kind of freedom and independence with which he may control his own actions. At the same time he still appears to feel quite accountable to others, particularly his father. He sometimes seems to feel the need to justify his actions, and he acts at times as if he felt himself observed and under scrutiny. All of this could be relevant here and to indicate to us a fairly strong emphasis upon this issue at the present time.

3. *Initiative vs. guilt,* Rating: 3.5. Guilt is expressed a number of times. Some of it is related to sexual matters. He describes qualms about intercourse and about "delving." There are also indications of guilt, partly coming from his relationship with father, centering around the question of how active, energetic, and successful he should be as opposed to being happy, easy going, ineffectual, and to leaving nothing behind as he seems to desire. A lack or inhibition of intrusiveness also seems to interfere significantly with the depth and activity of his thinking. The interview itself is rather unreflective, shallow, and lacking in manifestations of curiosity or sustained interests. Thus, manifestations of this issue are fairly prominent in the record.

4. *Industry vs. inferiority,* Rating: 3. This issue is to be judged in terms of the degree to which the subject adopts the cultural definitions and requirements for production and emphasizes the skills and techniques related to that production in his life. In our subject's life work assumes a relatively minor role; he seems to be as reluctant to become seriously involved or committed to it as he is in his relation to people or to abstract issues. Relevant here is also his almost emphatic protestation that it is unnecessary to leave anything behind in the world. His hedonistic orientation similarly seems to imply a rejection of productive skills and roles. To a degree it would also seem that his reluctance to create and to produce has implications for the issue of generativity to be discussed later. The material does not allow us to come to a conclusion concerning the question whether his dislike to commit himself to productive work and to give it a

major share of his thoughts is the result of some lacking confidence which our subject may experience concerning his own productive capacity.

5. *Identity vs. identity diffusion,* Rating: 4. The subject repeatedly emphasizes his uncertainty about his future in terms of career, of heterosexual relationships, and of his own self-definition. In some phases of his life, such as that spent in Hawaii, his hedonistic emphasis seemed to imply an almost active avoidance of any personal commitment. The careers he is considering are quite divergent and do not seem to stem from any particularly strong or coherent interest pattern. The diffuseness of much of his ego orientation seems further manifested in his ambivalent and sometimes contradictory political and philosophical opinions as well as in their shallowness. Some aspects of his sexual identity appear to be similarly unsettled; we have previously discussed some possible underlying feminine trends in his identification. His repeated insistence upon not leaving anything behind in the world also seems to betray a certain sense of lacking definition of the self as well as a lack of desire to perpetuate it in any form. However, the subject seems, at least at times, to be concerned with his unsettledness and to wonder about his place in the world. Sometimes he appears to be mildly bothered by his sense of uncertainty concerning the future. On the whole, then, the issue of identity appears to dominate much of the patient's functioning at the present time.

6. *Intimacy vs. isolation,* Rating: 3. Manifestations of this issue are frequent in the interview. His relations to his parents appear to be characterized by a fair amount of distance; there seems to be little personal communication between him and them. His relationship to his father about which he tells us more than about that with his mother, seems to be dominated more by awe and some subordination than by mutuality and warmth. He has some difficulties in establishing close relationships with peers and particularly with girls, although he wishes strongly for a good "we" feeling. His previously discussed preference for a "dumb" wife whom he could dominate also would seem to reflect his inhibition of intimacy. Relevant also are his comments concerning sex and intercourse which express discomfort and anxiety in relation to these matters as well as his inquiries near the end of the

interview concerning how one might acquire the ability to love.

7. *Generativity vs. stagnation,* Rating: 2.5. This issue should be considered with the subject's age, as discussed before, in mind. Relevant evidence is found in the subject's already much quoted insistence on not leaving anything behind in the world and on not making any impact on it. There is his lack of interest in production, achievement, or in making any specific contributions. Marriage and having children are issues particularly absent from his thinking about the future. Again the question must be raised whether all these observations do not mostly reflect earlier issues, such as that of industry and whether because of the subject's age and developmental level the dimension of generativity can really be meaningfully applied to him.

## H. Character Elaborations

### 1. *Narcissistic,* Rating: 4

The definition of this scale seems to characterize the subject quite well. Egocentricity is certainly manifested in his wish to be admired but also in his self-centered hedonistic attitude; in his conviction that there is no need for him to contribute anything; and in his difficulties or inability to establish deeper relationships with other people. We saw his concern as well as his difficulties in loving others or in sharing more deeply common interests with others. There is evidence that he can get along with others but that he does so most probably in a rather superficial and shallow manner. His interest in others, his ability to give, to respond, to establish ties, and to return affection seem quite limited. Thus, a narcissistic orientation would seem to be quite predominant in this case.

### 2. *Hysterical,* Rating: 1.5

There may be some minor indications of hysterical trends in the form of some infantility, some Pollyannism, and some occasional, minor phobic reactions, particularly in sexual contexts. Other hysterical characteristics, however, are relatively lacking.

Thus, although his thinking is often rather shallow, he does not show outright hysterical naïveté. And the tendency to sexualize interpersonal relationships, so strongly emphasized in the definition of the scale, is fairly absent. Similarly the kind of repudiation of reality and the amount of wishful thinking implied in the definition are present in only minor degrees in the subject. Thus, a low rating seems indicated.

### 3. *Obsessive*, Rating: 1

The obvious lack of extensive or intensive thinking, his tendency to be easy going and unprecise, and to take the daily issues of his life very much for granted, as well as his minimal concern with formalisms, with ideals, or with strong rigid standards, all would seem to counterindicate a significant obsessive trend.

### 4. *Feminine-masculine*, Rating: 2 (feminine)

There are no strong indications of passive, tender, nurturant, or caring trends nor of strikingly feminine interests. We do observe his narcissistic and somewhat vain interest in his body, in how he looks in a bathing suit, and his scrutiny of himself in the mirror. In his attitude towards girls and sex he sometimes seems to take a position implying more than usual empathy with women. Also, when asked to describe an ideal person he mentions his brother's girl friend rather than a masculine figure.

### 5. *Dependent*, Rating: 2

Little dependency is expressed by the subject in relation to his parents. Somewhat more seems to appear in relation to age mates and peers, and perhaps also to girls. While, as we observed repeatedly, he seems to have some difficulties in establishing more deeply empathic relationships, he nevertheless seems to need the presence of others and finds it hard to get along without it. On the other hand, there are no major signs that the subject makes active efforts to find people to depend on. One might speculate from the previously mentioned inferences concerning a deep sense of uprootedness and of depression that the subject's confidence in finding others to depend on essentially, is somewhat limited.

### 6. *Sado-masochistic,* Rating: 1

While we find that the subject on occasion is able to become angry or furious, and to experience resentment, a major acting-out of aggressive drives or of wishes to be victimized does not seem to be a part of his general character make-up.

### 7. *Passive-aggressive,* Rating: 1.5

There is minimal evidence of passive-aggressive behavior or attitudes. There are some indications that away from home the subject acts in certain ways or does things (including smoking and cursing) which he would not dare to do in the presence of his parents. While one may speculate that his happy-go-lucky orientation to life represents partly a reaction to his perfectionistic, achievement-oriented, and active father, such a reaction might not necessarily be best characterized as passive-aggressive.

### 8. *Hypomanic,* Rating: 2

Relevant here is especially the subject's general careless optimism which seems to derive, at least in part, from his use of denial as a prominent ego defense. His mildly ruthless wishes for foot-loose travel, for making new contacts, and for enjoying himself also may add to what can be considered a hypomanic trend. All these features, on the other hand, do not seem to add up to a consolidated, hypomanic character pattern.

### 9. *Schizoid,* Rating: 1

Almost all the characteristics of this form of character variation are absent in the subject's personality. The one mildly applicable one could be his relative distance in object relationships. This, however, can also be conceptualized in terms of narcissism and was used as a partial basis for our rating of that variable.

## 10. *Projective,* Rating: 1

Again none of the criteria contained in the definition of this category seem applicable. One might speculate whether the subject's naïve trustfulness and optimism could be in part the result of a denial of suspicious and distrustful trends. But evidence for such trends, which might perhaps appear on deeper levels as approached by psychological tests, is minimal in this interview record.

## 11. *Psychopathic,* Rating: 2

While this rating reflects some tendency of psychopathy, it is not based on evidence of any tendency in the subject to get in trouble with the law or to act-out in any antisocial manner. Rather, it is intended to reflect mild indications of selfish manipulativeness on the subject's part. In describing his work in the dining hall, for instance, he emphasizes ingratiating himself with his supervisors, and getting by with just enough work to avoid being fired. Similarly, in his summer employment he strove to be maximally accepted with a minimum of personal effort. In leading others he also seems more oriented toward gaining their favor than toward carrying out a program reflecting his own convictions.

## 12. *Diffusion,* Rating: 3

Several features point to a lack of a more permanent pattern of life and of character, at least as it is established so far. Among them is his uncertainty as to what to do in the future: there is a question of marking time, of perhaps going into the army since so far he has found no appealing job. His occupational plans also lack consistency. Forest ranger, teacher, or big businessman all imply different qualifications as well as satisfactions. His ideologies are vague and do not supply him with specific and value-charged goals. His opinions are sometimes contradictory: he states in one place that he is afraid he might become a conservative, while in another place he designates himself as being such at present.

### 13. *As-if*, Rating: 1

Although some lack of depth and of genuineness and integration is indicated, this is not significant enough to suggest a major "as-if" quality of his character structure.

### 14. *Counterphobic*, Rating: 2

We find the subject describing a good deal of liking for rough sports (he likes games "the rougher the better, as far as I'm concerned the greatest game on earth would be no penalties") and for driving fast and dangerously even though he reports mild fear in doing the latter. In a similar vein he sometimes seems to like to tease and provoke his father's anger by confronting the latter with minor infractions of rules. Thus he seems to play with fear—or anxiety-arousing situations, apparently enjoying his mastery of them. Again, however, this counterphobic trend is no more than a tendency and it does not represent a major character pattern.

### 15. *Depressive*, Rating: 2

Throughout the record we find manifestations of a sense of feeling moderately unloved and lonely. A good deal of the subject's effort seems to go into attempts to achieve status and a position of being wanted by others. At the same time it may well be that the independent and rather off-hand position he sometimes seems to assume with girls is born of a fear over possibly being rejected. In one statement he accuses his mother of favoring the brother; while this certainly reflects some sibling rivalry it also seems to convey a depressive feeling of missing-out. His wish to avoid leadership positions because of their isolation also seems relevant as might be the frequently referred-to hedonistic attitude which could imply a need for satisfaction stemming from a sense of more basic deprivation.

### 16. *Genital*, Rating: 1.5

While none of the characteristics enumerated in the definition of this category seem completely absent, it also seems clear that most of them are so far only rather minimally developed in the subject. Most of what has been said under previous headings is relevant here and forms the basis for the rating given.

Again, as we did before in the case of subject A, we will attempt to summarize some of the main recurrent characterological themes which appear to pervade the entire constellation of ratings on the separate dimensions of the assessment scheme.

In his relations to others and toward the world in general subject B, at least on the surface, presents a markedly optimistic and trusting attitude. He is involved with others, is self-confident, and lacks self-consciousness, shame, or a sense of frustration. His trusting orientation is also indirectly expressed in the noteworthy absence of projectiveness or suspiciousness. Yet it appears that this openness and emotional and social responsivity has a somewhat shallow and superficial quality. The orientation of trust seems at times almost exaggeratedly emphasized. In his more basic structure, subject B shows, as expressed in the cluster of some ratings, a rather marked lack of internal consolidation and definition. He is described as being diffuse in his ego identity, basically nonintimate and isolated, and as stagnating and, so far, incapable of significantly generative behavior. This theme is also manifested in his high ratings on the character elaborations of narcissism and diffusion.

His shallowly trusting orientation which, so to speak, nevertheless extends through a considerable breadth of his relations, appears to be maintained largely by the indicated, rather heavy reliance on the defense mechanism of denial. This tendency to deny and to pretend that everything is more or less fine in the way it is, however, seems also to contribute to some relative reduction of inner depth. Here we find a similar effect as in the case of subject A but within a generally quite different constellation of factors. Subject B, although he shows some at least moderate strength of affects, nevertheless thinks shallowly, is minimally original, and his capacity for controlled, constructive, and productive regression is quite limited. There are few signs of positive, defined, and characterologically institutionalized strengths. His superego is rated as somewhat weak, and, consistent with the general pattern of diffusion, there seems to be a good deal of fluidity in the characteristics of his functioning which in part may be retained with the purpose of pleasing others.

Again this is hardly a complete description of the major dynamic trends of importance. Our aim here is only to illustrate the interdependence, intra- or interindividual, of the various dimensions on which ratings are made. It is important to note at this point also that such configurational descriptions derived from constellations of ratings yield only data concerning *formal* aspects of functioning. *Content* data have to be drawn from the diagnostic material on which the ratings originally were based.

# 6

## STATISTICAL DATA

After the scales in the Characterological Assessment Scheme had been developed, a number of test protocols and interview records of different subjects were rated during a pilot study. In this period of experimentation our raters, including the authors, acquired experience with the scheme, but we also still felt free to sharpen the definitions of the scales or to reword some of the criteria for the different scale steps when necessary. Following this pilot period we began to use the scheme for the collection of research data. After the ratings of test protocols and interview records of a first group of subjects had been completed we subjected them to statistical analyses in order to obtain information concerning the discrimination and the reliability of the scales. This information, based on the separate test and interview ratings of 19 volunteer subjects, normal Yale freshmen, is reported in the following paragraphs. It should be kept in mind that the ratings which were subjected to the various analyses, had been made by investigators familiar and experienced with the use of the scheme and reasonably homogeneous in their theoretical orientation as well as being well trained in the interpretation of clinical psychological tests. The kinds of test and interview data on which the ratings were based are well illustrated by those reported in the case studies in the preceding chapter. Subjects A and B actually are members of the group of 19 referred to above.

A number of steps were taken, as part of our research procedure, to avoid contamination of raters and ratings. Test data and interviews were rated separately, the former by two, the latter in many instances by three independent judges. None of the judges had interviewed or tested the subjects whose material he was assessing. Test and interview protocols, furthermore, were coded in such a manner that the judges, who rated each kind of information at different periods, had no way of identifying the proper combinations of test and interview data.

### Discrimination of the Rating Scales

In order to be useful, the rating scales obviously must discriminate between at least some subjects. A scrutiny of the ranges over which the ratings on each scale extend yields some relevant information. Since the lowest possible rating on all scales is *1* and the highest is *5* in most cases (with the exception of C-8, D-2, and H-13), the greatest possible range of ratings on any of the scales is 4. Table 1 indicates how many of the scales show various ranges of ratings. The total number of scales is only 73 since C-8, D-2, H-13, G.A-7, and G.B-7 were omitted. The latter two were found not to be applicable in this group in any meaningful manner because of the relatively young age of our subjects.

**Table 1.  Number of Scales Showing Various Ranges of Ratings**

| Ranges | 1.5 | 2 | 2.5 | 3 | 3.5 | 4 | n |
|---|---|---|---|---|---|---|---|
| Tests | 2 | 14 | 17 | 24 | 12 | 4 | 73 |
| Interviews | 3 | 13 | 29 | 22 | 5 | 1 | 73 |

To compute these ranges the distributions of ratings by the two judges (of tests) and the three (of interviews) were combined. This seemed a justifiable procedure since inspection showed these distributions to be approximately normal and the means of the distributions of different raters were not, in general, very different. Between the judges of the test data these means differed, on the average, by less than $\frac{1}{5}$ of a scale point. The greatest differences between any two of the three judges of interview data varied around $\frac{1}{3}$ of a scale point.

The width of the distributions of ratings is not equally great for the major groupings of scales in the assessment scheme. Table 2 gives the mean ranges of ratings from groups A to H of the scales.

**Table 2.  Mean Ranges of Ratings on Scales in the Major Groups**

| Scale Group | A | B | C | D | E | F | G.A | G.B | H | Over-all Mean |
|---|---|---|---|---|---|---|---|---|---|---|
| Tests | 3.4 | 2.7 | 3.0 | 2.0 | 3.0 | 2.7 | 2.3 | 2.5 | 2.6 | 2.8 |
| Interviews | 2.4 | 2.5 | 2.8 | 1.8 | 2.4 | 2.4 | 2.6 | 2.9 | 2.5 | 2.6 |

It is also of relevance to observe how often extreme ratings of *1* or *5* were used on the different scales. Considering only test ratings, we find that ratings of *1* were given once or more on 24 scales, ratings of *5* on 15 scales, while on 4 scales ratings of *1* as well as of *5* occurred. Among the ratings of interview material we found that ratings of *1* were given on 27 scales, ratings of *5* on 5 scales, and on one scale ratings of *1* as well as *5* occurred.

The following conclusions are suggested by these data: a. Despite the relatively extreme definitions of many of the scale-steps numbered as *1* or *5*, and despite the fact that our subjects are drawn from a normal, not clinically extreme population, many scales are used in their full range. b. Tables 1 and 2 both show that, although the full range of *4* is not very often utilized, ratings on the whole are fairly widely distributed on most of the scales. It should be kept in mind that half-point ratings were as frequently made as ratings that correspond to the defined scale-steps represented by whole numbers. Thus, in practice, half-point intervals are perfectly meaningful. Further inspection of the data given so far indicated that ratings of interview data were consistently not quite as widely distributed over the scales as were ratings of test data. This is true even though the tables are based on data from three judges who might *a priori* be expected to show greater variation in their combined ratings than would only two. The smaller variation (and thus discrimination) of the scales appearing in our interview ratings must be kept in mind in evaluating the reliability data to be presented next.

*Reliability Data*

A simple, over-all measure of the reliability with which ratings are made on our scales is provided by percentages of agreement between two judges rating material obtained from the same subject. We defined two ratings on a given scale, made independently by two judges, as being in agreement if they differed by no more than half a point. In the cases of a split rating we counted it as half an agreement if the judges agreed on at least one part of their ratings. By this method percentages of agreement between two judges are obtained for each subject. Agreement on the test ratings varied, over the 19 subjects, between 51 and 82 per cent with a mean of 69 per cent. Agreement on ratings based on interviews varied between 57 and 86 per cent with a mean of 68 per cent. (More recently made ratings of further groups of subjects consistently show percentages of agreement in the mid-70's.) The difference between percentages of agreement on test ratings and interview ratings seems insignificant unless one considers the greater variation of test-based ratings on the scales in general. Thus, for our materials and our judges, ratings based on tests were probably somewhat more reliable than ratings based on interview data. The reason for this may be due in part to the fact that the specific relevance of certain test data to certain theoretical variables, especially those representing various ego functions, has been worked out in more detail (Schafer, 1954) than has been done for interview data.

The reliability of each separate scale was investigated by a different method. It was argued that the ratings of two judges on a given scale, were they distributed purely at random, could yield 81 possible pairs (including half-point ratings). Of these, 25 would by chance fulfill the criterion of agreement within half a point; the remaining 56 would represent disagreements. If these proportions are adjusted according to the number of our subjects, we obtain a theoretical, expected distribution for agreements and disagreements of the two judges on each scale. If the null-hypothesis is true, this distribution should be approximated by the actual data. The frequencies of agreement and disagreement actually observed were tested for each scale, and separately for test and for interview ratings, by means of chi-square. Corrections for continuity were applied.

Considering first the data derived from test ratings we find that agreement on ratings between two judges, significantly different from chance on the .01 level, exists on 47 scales; agreement significant on only the .05 level on 15 more scales. Thus 62 of the 78 scales could be used with good reliability. For interview ratings the findings are less satisfactory. On 23 scales agreement significant on the .01 level was reached, for another 23 on the .05 level; 32 scales were judged less reliably. The scales on which ratings were done with insignificant agreement on both tests and interviews are: B-5, E-6a, G.A-3, G.B-4, G.B-6, H-3, H-4, H-11, and H-12. Should these scales be eliminated? For the present we decided to retain them. Criteria for judging material relevant to these variables may yet be refined; furthermore, the scales even in their present form may possibly prove useful with different populations of subjects.

Thirty-nine scales, exactly half of the complete set, were judged reliably at least at the .05 level on the basis of both test and interview material. These are: A-1, A-2, B-2, B-6, C-1, C-2, C-3, C-6, C-7, C-8, D-1, D-2, E-3, E-4, E-5b, E-6b, E-7a, E-7b, E-7c, E-8a, E-8b, E-8c, E-8d, E-9, F-1, F-3, F-6, G.A-1, G.A-4, G.B1, G.B2, H-6, H-7, H-8, H-9, H-13, H-15, and H-16. In the cases of C-8, D-2, and H-16 the high interjudge agreement seems to be due to the relative lack of discrimination of the scales for the population of our subjects. Actually C-8 and D-2 each have only a few defined scale steps. For all other scales the range of scale steps made use of by raters is at least 2, that is 4 half-points, on either test or interview ratings.

In general, then, it seems fair to conclude that the rating scales contained in the characterological assessment scheme here presented show, on the whole, adequate discrimination and, in the case of most of them, acceptable reliability, even for the relatively restricted and homogeneous population of subjects used. Agreement on the over-all description of subjects, using all the scales, as reflected in percentages of agreement, also seems sufficient for practical purposes of assessment.

A question which cannot be fully treated here concerns not the assessment scheme but the subjects: Should we expect assessment ratings of tests and interview material obtained from the same subjects to agree? This is a problem involving levels of personality, and the degrees and kinds of integration of those levels we think we may have to expect. Actually, among the student subjects whose data are utilized here, we found very high agreement (significant on at least the .02 level) between ratings based on tests and ratings based on interview in 7 out of 19 cases. For the other subjects agreement is less marked; in a few instances the two sets of ratings approach almost random co-variation. Problems such as these seem primarily to represent issues of personality theory and assessment methodology. And agreements between test and interview ratings in these seven cases have no simple explanation; these subjects are neither more "abnormal" or otherwise conspicuous, nor are their ratings particularly extreme.

An interesting issue, which cannot be further pursued here, concerns the possibility that the reliability with which certain aspects of a person's functioning can be rated, is in itself to some degree a function of that person. Even in daily life we distinguish "predictable" from "unpredictable" people. In terms of some of the scales of the scheme we might ask whether rigid, or obsessive individuals, or those with well-established ego identities, for instance, can be rated more reliably than diffuse or immature or "as-if" personalities. Further research using our scheme may throw some light on these questions.

# 7
# OTHER APPLICATIONS

In the two illustrative case presentations given above we exemplified the rating procedure, as applied to test and interview records, by utilizing the entire set of 78 scales. This manner of using the assessment scheme, yielding a fairly comprehensive *assessment-of* an individual character structure, represents only one of several possible ways of applying the scales. Modifications of the illustrated procedure can be made by rating information different from test or interview records. Thus it is possible, for instance, to use the scheme for a frame of reference for a sophisticated "mental status" examination based on case records and diagnostic interviews, or to subject therapeutic interviews, whether individual or in group settings, to scrutiny in terms of the different variables. Another possible form of modifying the use of the scheme is that of utilizing only some scales in various combinations for specific purposes. Thus, if one is particularly interested in ego defenses, the 11 scales dealing with "Prominent Defenses" may be extracted and used; the same may be done with any of the seven other major categories. Or if one is interested in evaluating issues represented by a specific combination of single scales, e.g., depression, elation, adequacy of reality testing or cognitive reactivity, only such a group of scales may be selected and applied to relevant diagnostic material. For particular purposes, when overall assessment is not necessary or desired and when the Gestalt quality of character can be neglected, even single scales could be used. Since some of the scales overlap considerably, a careful selection of only certain scales may at times imply only a moderate loss of information.

On occasion it may also be useful to combine certain scales to form new ones. The authors have experimented with such procedures for certain aspects of their research although not for purposes of over-all assessment. Thus, from the five scales making up "Ideational Styles," one single scale has been derived that ranges from "active" to "constricted." The same was done for the eight scales of the Affect category: these were combined into a single five-point rating scale ranging from "optimum adaptive affect" to "substantial affect disturbance." Similar procedures can be easily followed especially within the categories of "Adaptive Strengths" and "Sense of Self."

One of the authors applied the assessment scales to the recorded verbalizations of four members participating in group therapy sessions. All scales were used with the exception of those in the categories of "Sense of Self" and "Psychosocial Modalities." Since the four group members had not previously been assessed by tests or interviews, no comparison with such ratings could be made. However, two scorers rating the group sessions independently achieved the following percentages of agreement, within half a point, on each of the four members: 58, 63, 68, and 77. The combined congruence of agreement within half a point was 66.7 per cent. These percentages of agreement are not very much lower than those achieved using individual interviews and psychological tests. A good deal of further work in this area is necessary, but the possibility of a third source of assessment data, that is, through records of group participation, is one that suggested itself in these studies.

In some instances it is possible to utilize the scales as dimensions serving the operational definition of a preconceived conceptualization concerning certain aspects of characterological functioning. Thus, in another part of our research we were interested in a classification of our subjects according to types of ego identity as derived from some of Erikson's writings. His descriptions of varieties of identity development suggested, theoretically, three major types which we labeled: 1. Normally developing, 2. Rigid, foreclosed, and 3. Diffuse, conflicted. From Erikson's statements concerning identity structures and development we next formulated brief theoretical definitions of each type. In abbreviated form they are the following:

1. A *normally developing* ego identity is characterized by the presence of a relatively dominant configuration of reasonably consistently integrated identity elements (such as prominent defenses, important identifications, outstanding impulses and motives, specifically dominant superego commands and restrictions, well-developed skills, specific social roles, etc.). Other available identity elements are only partly or not at all integrated into this configuration but their existence is subjectively recognized and acknowledged and some flexible experimentation with them can be observed. There is some stability to the existing identity configuration but it is open to some modification and no extreme defensive processes are set in operation to keep it intact in exactly its existing form.

2. A *rigid or foreclosed* ego identity is dominated by a relatively small number of strongly emphasized identity elements such as single defenses, superego commands or restrictions, specific values, etc. These identity elements are integrated into a narrow, fairly inflexible, and usually rather emphatically defended identity configuration from which significant other elements, which are potentially available, are actively excluded. Often there prevails a sort of overly pervasive integration and homogenization of the elements included into the narrow identity configuration which concomitantly may lose subtlety and complexity.

3. In the *diffuse, conflicted* identity type we find various distinguishable identity elements but no dominant, significant, or stable synthesis of them. These elements may enter various, sometimes rather short-lived configurations which are more or less easily dissolved and differently recombined again. In other cases we may find more or less acute conflict between various identity elements or sub-configurations of them. Synthetic efforts may be  made continually by the person's ego but are often hampered by the contradictory contents and demands of various identity elements. Sometimes personalities with diffuse and conflicted identities may appear to be particularly rich and colorful while in other instances they may present more ominous pictures of disturbance or of developmental arrest.

In order to develop a set of criteria for coordinating individual subjects to the three theoretically derived identity groups we scrutinized each scale in the assessment scheme for its relevance to the three definitions. Whenever a scale was found relevant, the definitions of each one of the scale steps were studied. Whenever different steps were found to be expressive of some aspect of each one of the three identity types, the scale was included in a list of criteria for identity typing. Only those scales were finally selected which seemed to contain steps applicable to each of the three types. There are 32 of them; the ratings felt to be representative of each of the three identity types were recorded and are presented in Table 3.

For reasons inherent in the design of the research for which this classification of identity types is used, only the ratings of test protocols obtained from our subjects were used as a basis for classifying them according to their identity type. All their ratings on the 32 scales selected were compared to the spans of ratings thought to be characteristic of each identity type and the frequency with which each subject's ratings fell into each type was recorded. It was arbitrarily decided to assign each subject to that group for which he had received the most tallies if there was a majority of at least two tallies over the identity group represented with second-greatest frequency. If there was no such clear majority (as proved to be the case with only a small proportion of subjects) the person was assigned to a "mixed" type.

This is not the place to describe the research on ego identity of which this classification procedure is a part but it may serve as another example of a way of using the assessment scheme. The three theoretically derived identity types are operationally defined in terms of clusters of scales and serve as an independent variable.

**Table 3.  Criterion Ratings on Assessment Scales for Three Identity Groups (n=32)**

| Category | Normally Developing | Rigid Foreclosed | Diffuse, Conflicted |
|---|---|---|---|
| A-1 | 2.5–3.5 | 1–2 | 4–5 |
| A-2 | 2.5–3.5 | 1–2 | 4–5 |
| A-3 | 2.5–3.5 | 1–2 | 4–5 |
| B-1 | 2.5–3.5 | 1–2 | 4–5 |
| B-5 | 2.5–3.5 | 1–2 | 4–5 |
| C-4 | 2–3 | 3.5–5 | 1–1.5 |
| C-6 | 1–2 | 2.5–3.5 | 4–5 |
| C-10 | 3.5–4 | 4.5–5 | 1–3 |
| D-2 | 1.5 | 1 | 2–3 |
| E-1 | 3.5–4 | 4.5–5 | 1–3 |
| E-2 | 3–4 | 4.5–5 | 1–2.5 |
| E-3 | 2.5–3.5 | 4–5 | 1–2 |
| E-4 | 2.5–3.5 | 4–5 | 1–2 |
| E-5a | 2.5–3.5 | 1–2 | 4–5 |
| E-5b | 3–4 | 1–2.5 | 4.5–5 |
| E-6b | 3–4 | 1–2.5 | 4.5–5 |
| E-7a | 3–4 | 1–2.5 | 4.5–5 |
| E-7c | 3–4.5 | 1–2.5 | 5 |
| E-8a | 3–4 | 1–2.5 | 4.5–5 |
| E-8c | 3–4 | 1–2.5 | 4.5–5 |
| E-9 | 3–4 | 4.5–5 | 1–2.5 |
| F-4 | 2–3.5 | 1–1.5 | 4–5 |
| G-A2 | 2.5–3.5 | 1–2 | 4–5 |
| G-A4 | 2–3 | 1–1.5 | 3.5–5 |
| G-A5 | 2–3 | 1–1.5 | 3.5–5 |
| G-B1 | 1–2 | 2.5–3.5 | 4–5 |
| G-B2 | 1–2 | 2.5–3.5 | 4–5 |
| G-B5 | 1–2 | 2.5–3.5 | 4–5 |
| H-1 | 1–1.5 | 2–3 | 3.5–5 |
| H-9 | 1–2 | 2.5–3.5 | 4–5 |
| H-12 | 1.5 | 1 | 2–5 |
| H-16 | 2.5–5 | 2 | 1–1.5 |

# REFERENCES

Abraham, K. (1921). Contributions to the Theory of the Anal Character. In *Selected Papers of Karl Abraham*. New York: Basic Books, 1953, pp. 370–392.

——— (1924). Influence of Oral Erotism on Character Formation. In *Selected Papers of Karl Abraham*. New York: Basic Books, 1953, pp. 393–406.

——— (1925). Character Formation on the Genital Level of the Libido. In *Selected Papers of Karl Abraham*. New York: Basic Books, 1953, pp. 407–417.

Allport, G. W. (1953). The Trend in Motivational Theory. *Amer. J. Orthopsychiat.*, 23: 107–119.

Burgess, E. W. and Cottrell, L. S. Jr. (1939). *Predicting Success or Failure in Marriage*. New York: Prentice-Hall.

Cronbach, L. J. (1956). Assessment of Individual Differences. In *Annual Review of Psychology*. ed. Farnsworth, P. R. and McNemar, Q. Stanford, Calif.: Annual Reviews, 7: 173–196.

Erikson, E. H. (1950). *Childhood and Society*. New York: Norton.

——— (1959). Identity and the Life Cycle. *Psychological Issues*, 1 (1). New York: International Universities Press.

Fenichel, O. (1945). *The Psychoanalytic Theory of Neurosis*. New York: Norton.

Freud, A. (1936). *The Ego and the Mechanisms of Defense*. New York: International Universities Press, 1946.

Freud, S. (1900). *The Interpretation of Dreams*. New York: Basic Books, 1958.

—— (1905). *Three Essays on the Theory of Sexuality*. Standard Ed. 7: 123–245. London: Hogarth Press, 1953.

—— (1908). Character and Anal Erotism. *Collected Papers, 2: 45–50*. London: Hogarth Press, 1950.

—— (1913a). The Excretory Functions in Psychoanalysis and Folklore. *Collected Papers, 5: 88–91*. London: Hogarth Press, 1950.

—— (1913b). The Predisposition to Obsessional Neurosis. *Collected Papers, 2: 122–132*. London: Hogarth Press, 1950.

—— (1915). Some Character-Types Met with in Psychoanalytic Work. *Collected Papers, 4: 318–344*. London: Hogarth Press, 1950.

—— (1916). On the Transformation of Instincts with Special Reference to Anal Erotism. *Collected Papers, 2: 164–171*. London: Hogarth Press, 1950.

—— (1917a). Mourning and Melancholia. *Collected Papers, 4: 152–170*. London: Hogarth Press, 1950.

—— (1917b). *A General Introduction to Psychoanalysis*. New York: Perma Giants, 1949.

—— (1923). *The Ego and the Id*. Standard Ed. *19: 12–66*. London: Hogarth Press, 1961.

—— (1926). *Inhibitions, Symptoms, and Anxiety*. London: Hogarth Press, 1949.

—— (1931). Libidinal Types. *Collected Papers, 5: 247–251*. London: Hogarth Press, 1950.

—— (1937). Analysis Terminable and Interminable. *Collected Papers, 5: 316–357*. London: Hogarth Press, 1950.

—— (1938). *Outline of Psychoanalysis*. New York: Norton, 1949.

Gardner, R., Holzmann, P. S., Klein, G. S., Linton, H., and Spence, D. P. (1959). Cognitive Control. *Psychological Issues, 1* (4). New York: International Universities Press.

Hartmann, H. (1939). *Ego Psychology and the Problem of Adaptation*. New York: International Universities Press, 1958.

—— (1950). Comments on the Psychoanalytic Theory of the Ego. *The Psychoanalytic Study of the Child, 5: 74–96*. New York: International Universities Press.

Hartmann, H., Kris, E., and Loewenstein, R. M. (1946). Comments on the Formation of Psychic Structure. *The Psycho-*

*analytic Study of the Child, 2:* 11–38. New York: International Universities Press.

Holt, R. R. (1958). Clinical and Statistical Prediction: A Reformulation and Some New Data. *J. abn. soc. Psychol., 56:* 1–12.

Holt, R. R. and Luborsky, L. (1958). *Personality Patterns of Psychiatrists.* 2 Vols. New York: Basic Books.

Jacobson, E. (1954). The Self and the Object World. *The Psychoanalytic Study of the Child, 9:* 75–127. New York: International Universities Press.

Jones, E. (1918). Anal-Erotic Character Traits. *J. abn. Psychol., 13:* 261–284.

Kelly, E. L. and Fiske, D. W. (1951). *The Prediction of Performance in Clinical Psychology.* Ann Arbor, Michigan: University of Michigan Press.

Klein, G. S. (1954). Need and Regulation. In *Nebraska Symposium on Motivation,* ed. Jones, M. Lincoln, Neb.: University of Nebraska Press, pp. 224–274.

Kris, E. (1952). *Psychoanalytic Explorations in Art.* New York: International Universities Press.

Meehl, P. E. (1954). *Clinical vs. Statistical Prediction.* Minneapolis, Minnesota: University of Minnesota Press.

Michaels, J. J. (1958). Character Disorder and Acting Upon Impulse. In *Readings in Psychoanalytic Psychology,* ed. Levitt, M. New York: Appleton, 1958.

Murray, H. A., et al. (1938). *Explorations in Personality.* New York: Oxford University Press.

Nunberg, H. (1931). The Synthetic Function of the Ego. In *Practice and Theory of Psychoanalysis.* New York: International Universities Press, 1955, pp. 120–136.

Office of Strategic Services, Assessment Staff, (1948). *Assessment of Men: Selection of Personnel for the Office of Strategic Services.* New York: Rinehart.

Paul, I. H. (1959). Studies in Remembering. *Psychological Issues, 1* (2). New York: International Universities Press.

Rapaport, D. (1951). The Autonomy of the Ego. *Bull. Menninger Clinic, 15:* 113–123.

——— (1957). Cognitive Structures. In *Contemporary Approaches to Cognition.* Cambridge, Mass.: Harvard University Press.

———— (1958). The Theory of Ego Autonomy: A Generalization. *Bull. Menninger Clinic, 22:* 13–35.

———— (1960). The Structure of Psychoanalytic Theory: A Systematizing Attempt. *Psychol. Issues, 2* (6): 1–158. New York: International Universities Press.

———— Gill, M., and Schafer, R. (1945–1946). *Diagnostic Psychological Testing.* Chicago: Year Book.

Reich, W. (1933). *Character-Analysis.* New York: Orgone Institute Press, 1949.

Sadger, J. (1910). Analerotik und Analcharakter. In *Die Heilkunde.*

Sarbin, T. R. (1943). A Contribution to the Study of Actuarial and Statistical Methods of Prediction. *Amer. J. Sociol., 48:* 593–603.

Schafer,, R. (1954). *Psychoanalytic Interpretation in Rorschach Testing.* New York: Grune and Stratton.

———— (1958). Regression in the Service of the Ego: The Relevance of a Psychoanalytic Concept for Personality Assessment. In Lindzey, G. *Assessment of Human Motives.* New York: Rinehart, 1958.

Simoneit, M. (1935). *Wehrpsychologie: Ein Abriss ihrer Probleme und praktischen Folgerungen.* Berlin: Bernard and Graefe.

Stern, G. G., Stein, M. I. and Bloom, B. S. (1956). *Methods in Personality Assessment.* New York: The Free Press of Glencoe.

Taft, R. (1959). Multiple Methods of Personality Assessment. *Psychol. Bull., 56:* 333–352.

Waelder, R. (1936). The Principle of Multiple Function: Observations on Overdetermination. *Psychoanal. Quart., 5:* 45–62.

# INDEX